I0902484

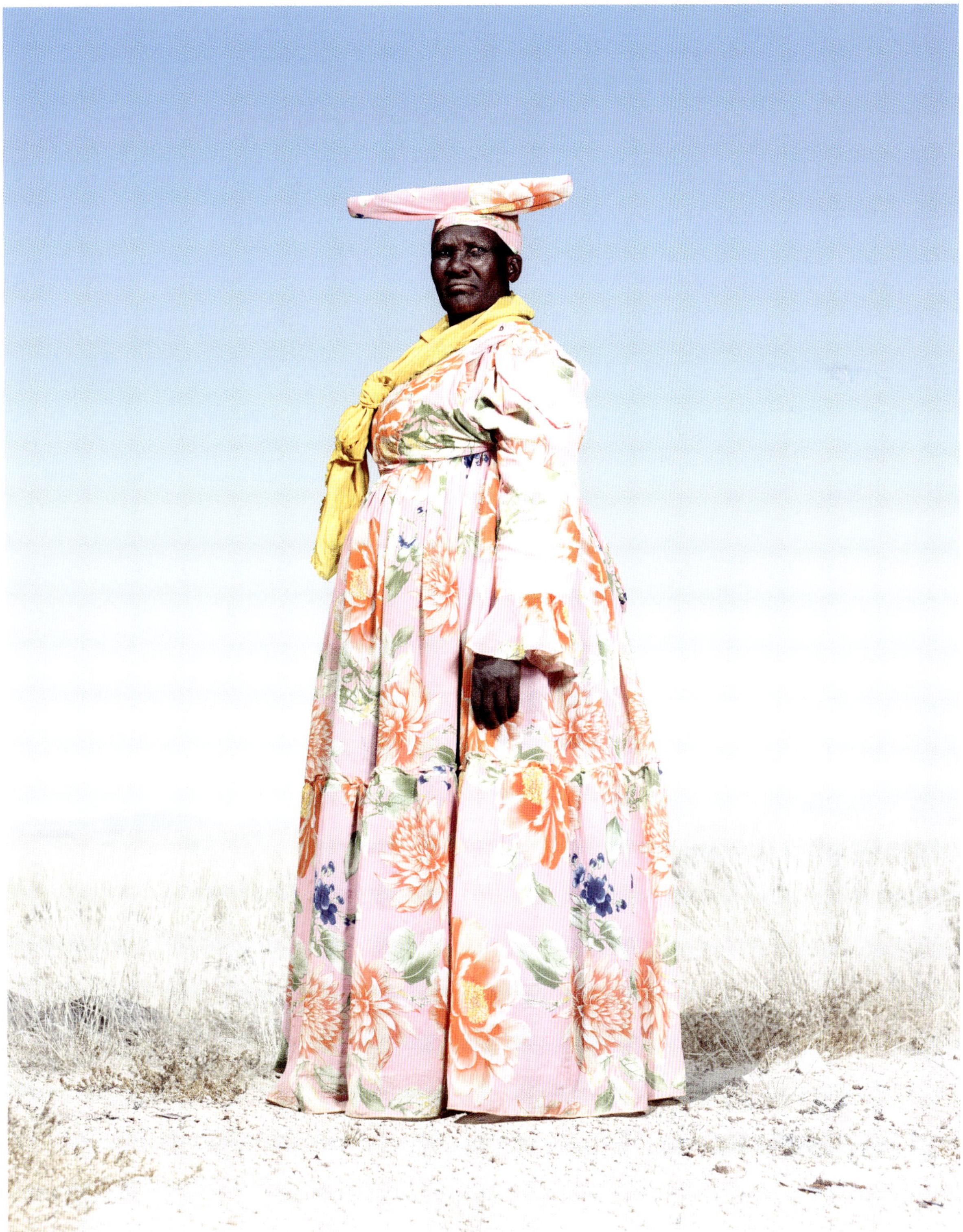

Conflict and Costume

The Herero Tribe of Namibia

Jim Naughten

Introduction by Lutz Marten

MERRELL
LONDON • NEW YORK

Contents

Preface

Jim Naughten

Crossing over the Orange River on an old and rusting 500cc motorbike, I felt as though I had been transported to a different planet: lunar, scorching and inhospitable. Barely a year out of college, I had only a rudimentary knowledge of Namibia and its people, but within a matter of days I had reached Lüderitz, a curiously out-of-place German colonial port, and visited Kolmanskop, a nearby German ghost town. I spent a few nights camped on the ominously named Shark Island, an island-turned-peninsula sandwiched between the dunes of the Namib Desert and the ice-cold waters of the Atlantic. (Years later, I would learn that it had been the site of a brutal concentration camp.) I was spellbound by the majesty and magnitude of the Namib, the world's oldest desert, and bewitched by Namibia's strangely elusive colonial history, little known or recorded, yet tantalizingly visible – superficially, at least – in the country's architecture, street names and deserted settlements, the last preserved only by the aridity of the desert.

I rode north, past the highest sand dunes in the world, towards the seaside resort of Swakopmund and the shipwreck-strewn Skeleton Coast, known as 'The Land God Made in Anger' by the local San tribe, in view of its isolated, desolate and hostile environment. Over the course of my travels, I learnt more about this remarkable corner of Africa, from the extraordinary cave paintings of the earliest inhabitants to the nomadic Himba people; and from the first Afrikaner settlers to its brief period as German South-West Africa and the days of the diamond rush. The incongruity of these images, with nomadic tribes, Teutonic architecture, ghost towns and iron crosses all set against a desert backdrop, gave me the impression that I had stumbled on to the set of a peculiar spaghetti western, full of anomalies and anachronisms, where the wrong buildings had been ordered and misplaced actors cast. The German–Herero war was only hinted at in the guidebooks and local museums.

In Swakopmund I caught sight of my first Herero woman, resplendent in brightly coloured patchwork dress and cow-horn headdress. She appeared to float along the promenade. Learning that this extraordinary and elegant clothing had its roots in the fashions of the Victorian era and the meeting of two vastly different cultures, I was hooked. Namibia was a country of contrasts and paradoxes – timeless, expansive and enchanting.

The story behind the clothing stayed with me, and more than a decade later I returned to Namibia to photograph the Herero people in earnest. This time I was able find more reading material on the early days of the Rhenish missionaries, the terrible German–Herero war, and its gruesome aftermath, which made the story all the more compelling. Why would this tribe wear the clothes and uniforms of the very people who had cost them so dearly?

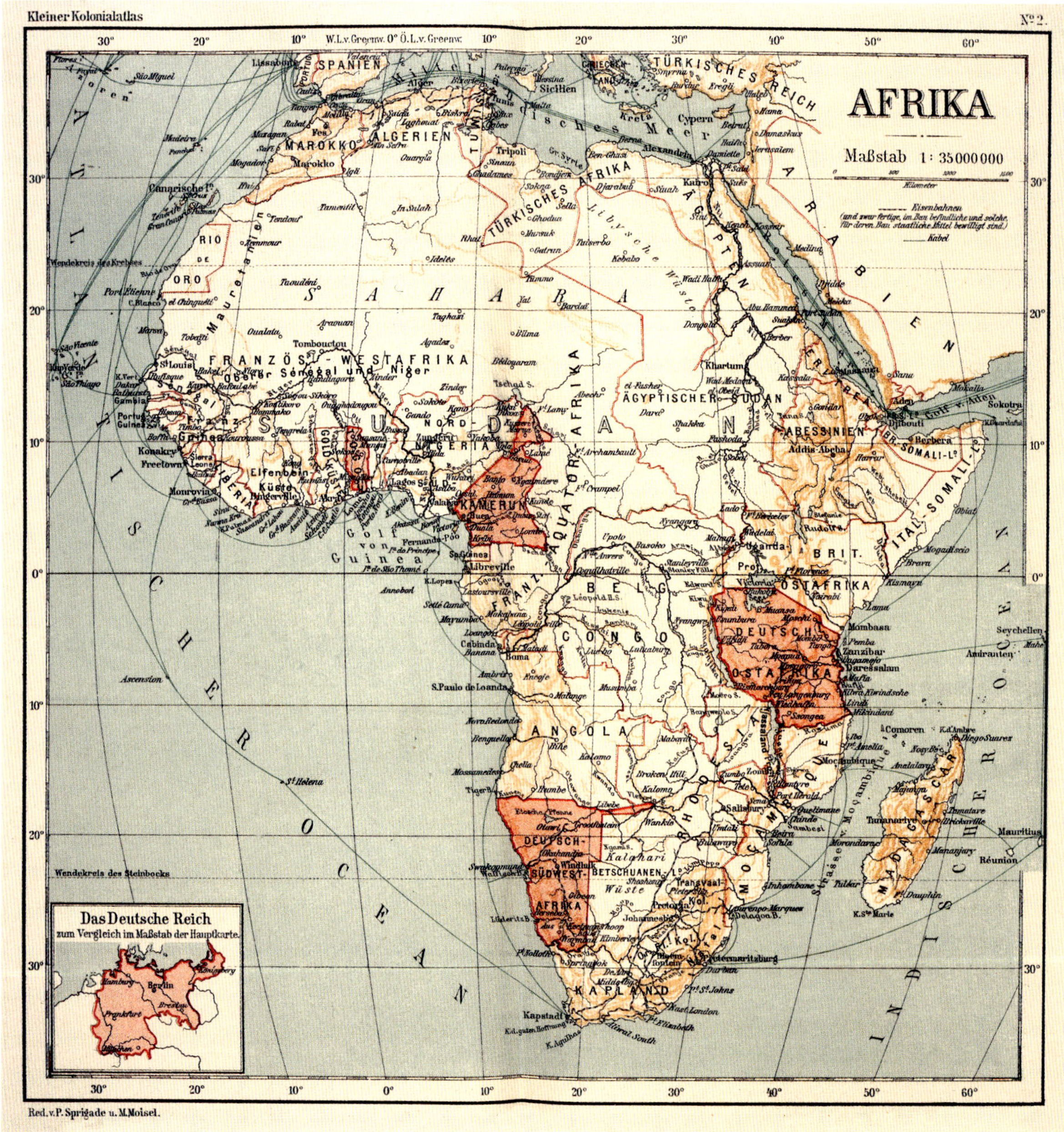

A map of Africa from 1910 showing, in red, the location of German colonies and, by means of an inset, their size relative to Germany; Namibia, then known as German South-West Africa, can be seen at the bottom of the continent. Taken from *Deutscher Kolonialatlas*, edited by P. Sprigade and M. Moisel, Berlin (Dietrich Reimer) 1910.

I travelled throughout Namibia, from the Namib Desert in the west to the Kalahari in the east, and from the Karas region in the south to Kaokoveld in the north, photographing at weddings, funerals, festivals, military parades and gatherings. I photographed against the expanse of the desert – using it as a backdrop – rather than in villages or towns, and used perspective and auxiliary lighting to imbue the images with the sense of timelessness, beauty and strength that I saw in the Herero people. The women have assimilated the dresses into Herero culture, adding colour, style and their distinctive and unique headdress to make them their own, a symbol of pride and status to the wearer. Likewise, the military uniforms worn by the men are often a far cry from either the first European-style uniforms introduced to the Herero or the battledress of the German colonial forces, while the 'troops' themselves, no longer a real army in any conventional sense, keep the history alive, honour their ancestors and act as a powerful symbol of defiance, survival and tribal identity. Perversely, they also serve as a ghostly portrait of the German troops and settlers who had such a profound impact on the Herero nation.

These portraits are not intended as a conventional record of Herero culture. They do not capture the subject in a snapshot of everyday life, nor with objects typical of routine or social standing. The subject's identity as a Herero tribe member is reified in their garments and their gaze, the vibrant colours brought into acute focus by the contrasting setting. In composing these portraits against the Namibian landscape – one of unforgiving intensity but also of silent witness – there is an enlivening that takes place in an otherwise frozen moment. The still space, a direct gaze, the re-appropriated clothes combine to create a stillness that allows the past to speak.

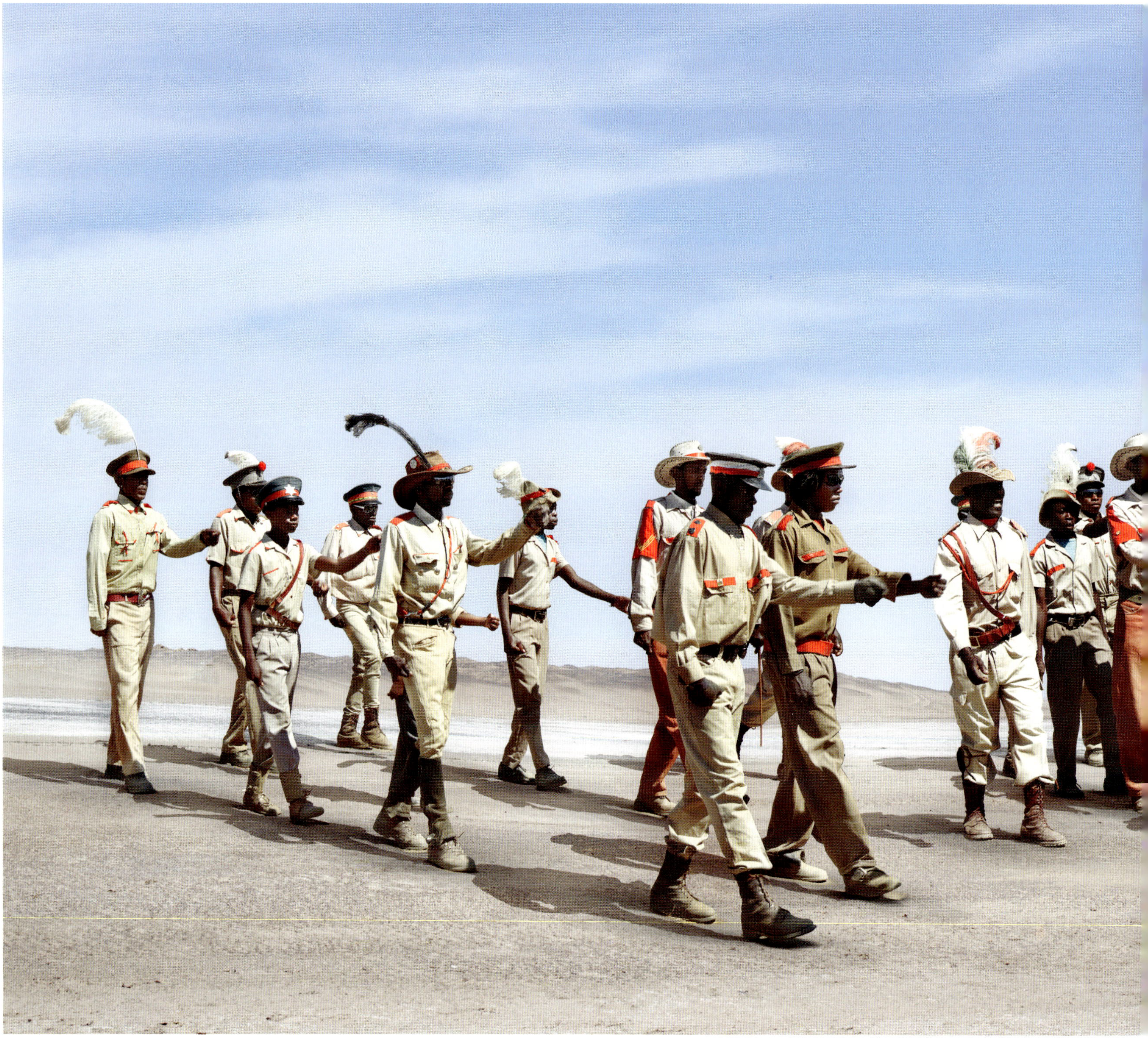

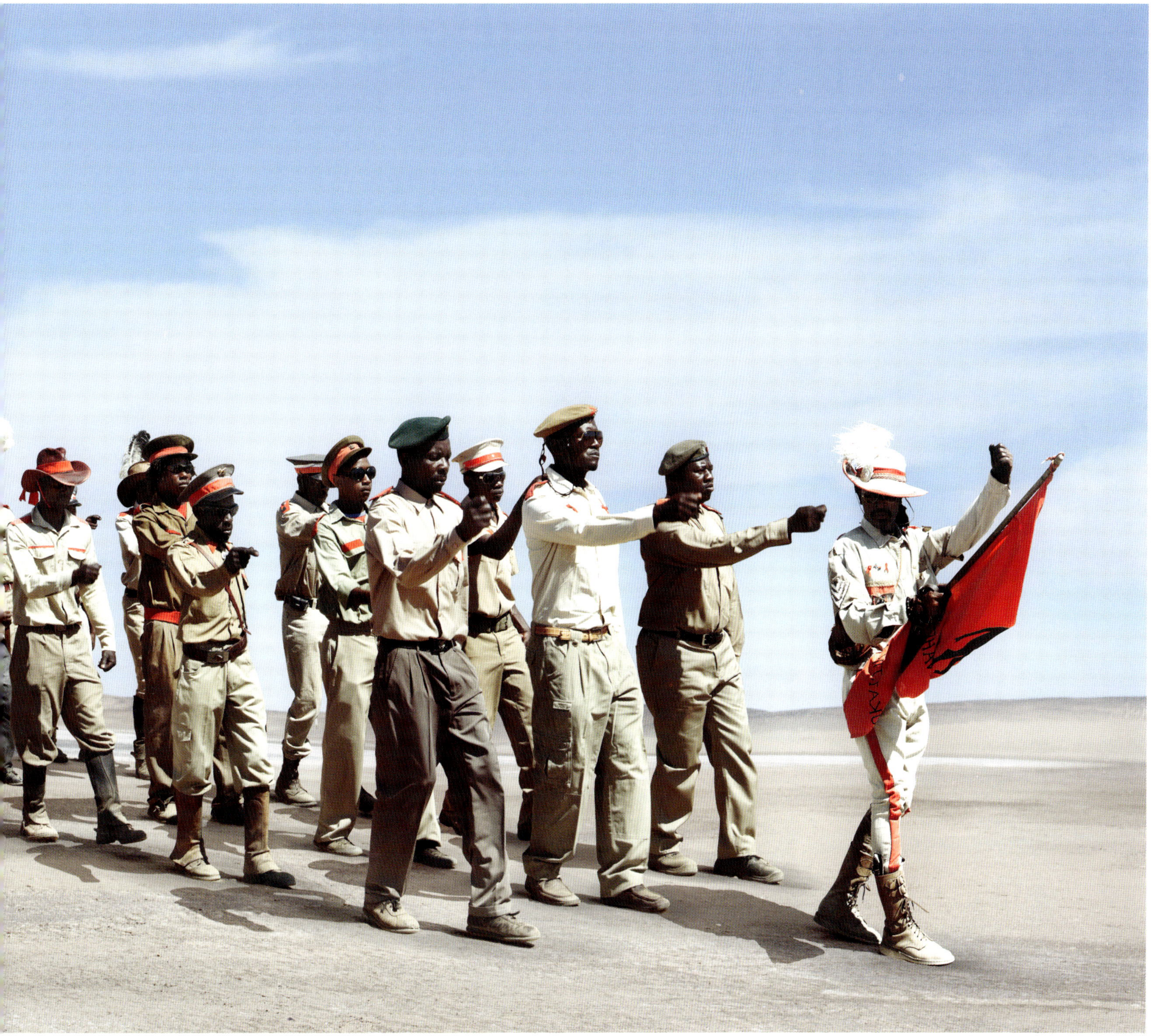

Introduction

Lutz Marten

The Herero (or *Ovaherero* in the Herero language) are an ethnic group of about 250,000 people living mainly in Namibia, with smaller groups in Angola to the north and Botswana to the east. In Namibia the Herero constitute approximately 10 per cent of the country's total population. Over the last 150 years, Herero society has undergone a series of profound changes – social, political and material – driven by the dynamics of innovation and of adaptation to both regional and global events. Interwoven into the dramatic and, at times, tragic history of modern Herero society is the story of the development of present-day Herero dress and dress codes: the male uniforms and female 'long dresses', and the emblematic red, green and white colour schemes. Both the uniforms and the long dresses have become part of a distinct Herero cultural identity, and are a well-known aspect of today's Namibian cultural heritage.

Although the exact origins of the Herero are not well documented, it is often proposed that Herero groups first entered northern and central Namibia in the eighteenth century. Herero society was historically composed of small, decentralized groups, while the economy was based on the raising of livestock, in particular cattle. Political and social leadership were organized around chiefs and a complex legal system of inheritance of wealth and power through both matrilineal and patrilineal descent.

From the 1850s onwards, the Herero came into increasing, and often hostile, contact with groups of Oorlam and Nama. These were Afrikaans- and Khoekhoe-speaking communities incorporating southern African Khoe people; freed labourers originally brought to the Cape Colony from India, Indonesia and other colonial territories; and individuals of mixed European, African and Asian ancestry. Migrating from the Cape, they entered southern Namibia and brought with them new commodities and ideas, from horses and ox-drawn wagons to guns and Christianity. They also brought new styles of clothing, and it was during these early days of contact with the wider world that the Herero were first introduced to military uniforms and Victorian-style dress. Uniforms were often given as presents to chiefs by traders (and later by colonial officials), and clothes and cloth became important articles of trade.

European mission stations, in particular of the German-based Rhenish Missionary Society, appeared around the same time, providing further access to the Cape and beyond. Increased exposure to different cultures coincided with internal changes to Herero society. Based on the backbone of the Herero economy – cattle – more centralized political and social structures developed, especially in the main Herero settlements in central Namibia, such as Okahandja, Omaruru and Otjimbingwe, where newly developing

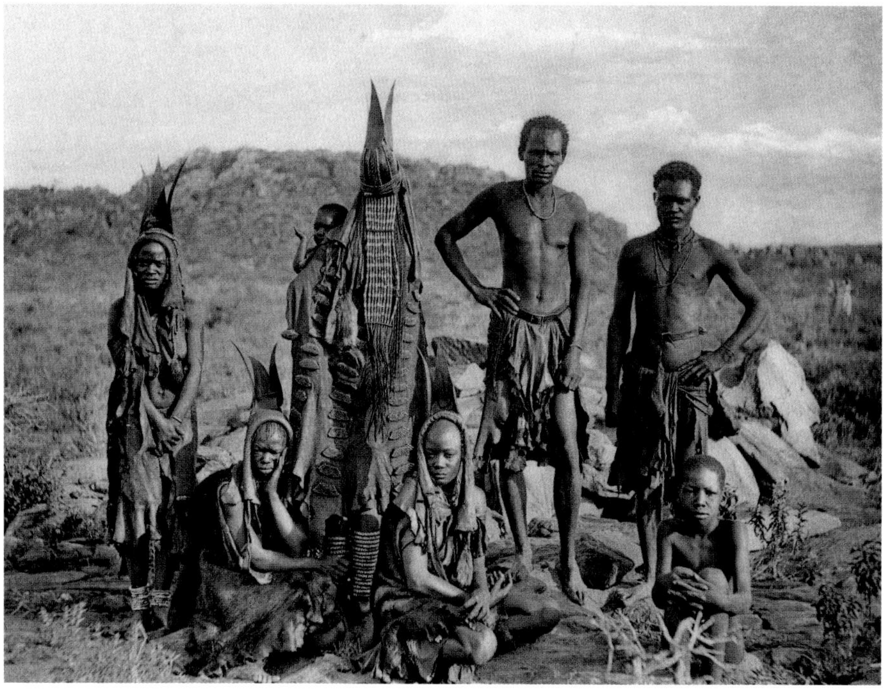

and expanding Herero chieftainships, trade and missionary activities were concentrated. Notably, well-to-do Herero men, especially those in the newly emerging regional centres, took to wearing trousers and suits.

Towards the end of the nineteenth century, Germany began to establish colonial rule in Namibia, which became German South-West Africa. German administration was often brutal and ruthless, and encompassed extreme notions of racial supremacy, whereby the country's original citizenship was to be either exterminated or turned into a soulless labour contingent. At the outset of German colonial rule, Herero chiefs adopted a dual strategy of exploitation of and resistance to the new arrivals and their political and economic aims. By early 1904, however, the situation had become bad enough for the Herero, under the leadership of Paramount Chief Samuel Maharero, to rise up against the colonizers, thus triggering the German–Herero war. Later that year, choosing not to confront the Herero forces in open battle, the German colonial army, the *Schutztruppe*, encircled the large number of Herero who had gathered on the Waterberg Plateau in north-central Namibia to discuss a strategy for future negotiations with the Germans, and, on 11 August, opened fire on men, women and children. Those who managed to escape the assault were forced into the Omaheke Desert, to die from hunger, thirst and exhaustion. During the following four years, both the Herero and

A group of Herero from the early German colonial period in a tableau arranged for the camera. The three-pronged leather headdress worn by the women was later replaced by the folded-cloth headdress worn by Herero women today. Both designs are symbolic representations of cattle horns.

the Nama, who had also fought the German colonialists, were persecuted, subjected to forced labour and interned in deathly concentration camps. The Herero and Nama genocide cost at least 60,000 lives, and left Herero society without land, without cattle and with damaged social and political structures.

German colonial rule in Namibia ended at the beginning of the First World War, when, in 1915, the *Schutztruppe* was defeated by South African forces. In the ensuing transition period, scattered Herero groups were quick to establish claims to their lost lands by settling at historical Herero sites, re-establishing communities and rebuilding their cattle herds. Although not committed to ethnic equality, the new administration was not entrenched enough to suppress these developments, and, in addition, was careful to distance itself from German atrocities in a bid to be awarded the territory at the end of the war, which indeed happened in 1918. The South African occupation of Namibia saw the establishment of Herero reservations, which provided a modest degree of independence and opportunities to pursue the raising of livestock.

Shortly after the end of the First World War, the *Otruppe* ('troops', 'army') movement gained momentum among the Herero, both male and female. (The movement is also sometimes called, in German, the *Truppenspieler*, meaning 'soldier players' or 'soldier actors'.) Members of the *Otruppe*, the antecedents of which can be traced back to the late nineteenth century,

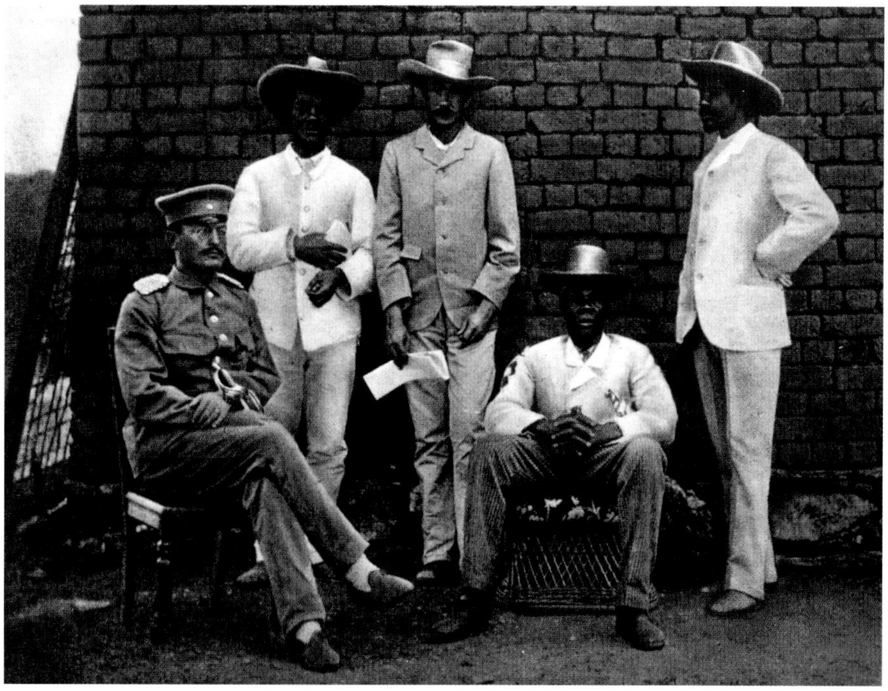

Herero chiefs Manasse Tjisista (seated, right) and Samuel Maharero (standing, far right) in a meeting with the colonial governor of German South-West Africa, Theodor Leutwein (seated, left), in Omaruru in 1896. Negotiations between the Germans and the Herero over trade, land and jurisdiction eventually gave way to confrontation and the German–Herero war.

created a national support network modelled on German military administrative structures, with local sections, top-down hierarchies and nationwide communication. Never conceived of as a military organization per se, the *Otruppe* nevertheless adopted the symbolism and practices of the military, including uniforms (often German uniforms captured from or left behind by the *Schutztruppe*); the use of military ranks and orders; exercising and marching; and ceremonial presence, especially at annual celebrations. With the establishment of the *Otruppe* movement, and in the wake of the German–Herero war and the end of German colonial rule, uniforms became increasingly important to Herero identity. The symbolism and insignia of German uniforms became obsolete, and so available for reinterpretation along Herero lines, while narratives provided the uniforms with new meaning; for example, that wearing the enemy's uniform will diminish their power and transfer some of their strength to the new wearer.

The *Otruppe* consists of three different sections, or 'flag movements': the *Otjiserandu* (Red Flag), the *Otjigrine* (Green Flag) and the *Otjizemba* (White Flag). The colour adopted by each section is central to its identity, and is reflected in the dress code of its members, with the *Otjizemba* using white dots on black. Here, too, narratives play an important role. The use of red in the hatbands, bandanas, epaulettes, buttons and dresses of the *Otjiserandu*, for example, is linked to the late nineteenth-century Herero wars with the Nama, during which a son of Chief Maharero Tjamuaha (Samuel Maharero's father) was accidentally killed by friendly fire. Rather than demanding retribution, the chief inaugurated the use of red hatbands to distinguish friend from foe – in particular, Herero from Witbooi Nama opponents, who wore white hatbands. Significantly, while in most military contexts a standardized uniform is important for identifying the wearer, it is less important among the Herero, for whom allegiance is signalled through the colour scheme – red, green or white – of the relevant flag movement. This combination of colour, unity and belonging is woven into the larger construction of Herero identity.

A key moment of modern Herero history, in which the *Otruppe* movement played a central part, was the funeral of Samuel Maharero. Following the German–Herero war, the paramount chief had fled with a group of Herero into Botswana, and had died there, in the town of Serowe, in March 1923. His body was returned to Namibia in August of that year, and an extensive funeral ceremony was held in Okahandja, the historical seat of the Maharero chieftainship, during which Samuel was buried next to his father. The celebration lasted for a week, and was attended by an unprecedented number of participants, including some 2500 uniformed and 170 mounted *Otruppe*

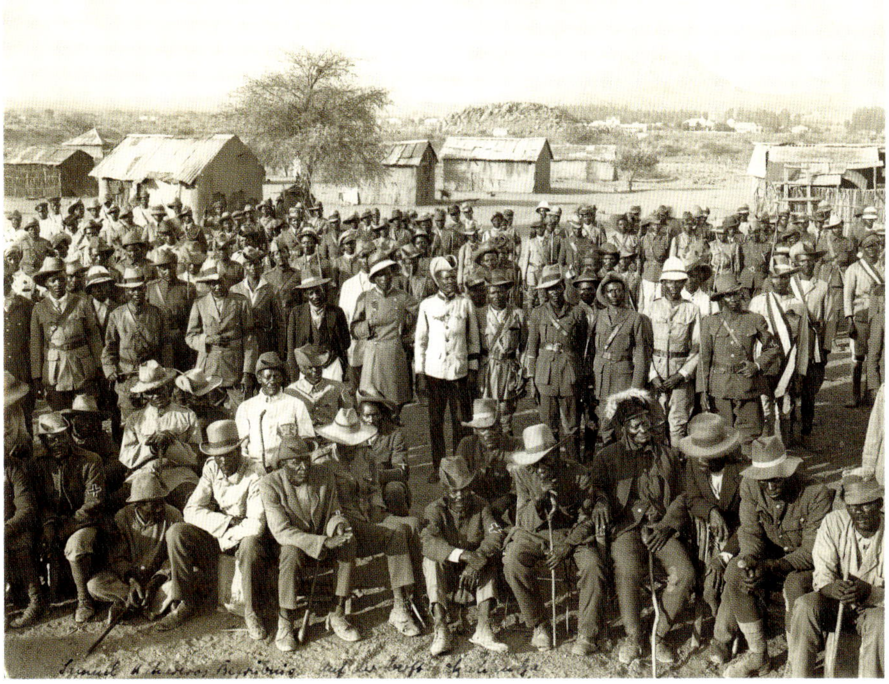

members. Men and women were dressed in uniforms and long dresses displaying the colour of the *Otjiserandu*, the section of the *Otruppe* most closely associated with the Maharero clan. The identificational value of such a display of unity and numbers was extremely high. It took place in one of the cultural and political centres of the historic Hereroland, then located in the middle of white-owned areas, and represented the ceremonial and symbolic reoccupation of tribal grounds. At the same time, it expressed a reunion with the past and the establishment of a new identity for the Herero community. The celebration has become an annual event – Herero Day, held every August – while several other annual ceremonies to commemorate chiefs have been established.

The three colour schemes of the *Otruppe* are especially prominent in the formal long dresses worn by the women. A red, green or white-dotted skirt – together with matching headdress, folded so as to resemble cow horns, and sometimes a matching cape – brings out the relevant colour scheme and creates the striking uniformity of marching groups of women at ceremonial occasions. While the men's uniforms are worn only at such special events (in other contexts, male attire consists of Western-style suits and hats), the women's long dress is also worn in everyday life, although here a wide variety of colours, as well as patchwork, is used. When the long dress became popular

Members of the *Otruppe* – many wearing German colonial uniforms, including the characteristic broad-brimmed hat with the brim turned up on one side – await the arrival of Samuel Maharero's coffin in Okahandja in 1923. The paramount chief's funeral was a landmark in the formation of post-First World War Herero identity.

among the Herero avant-garde during the early days of contact with the Cape, it replaced more traditional leather clothing; although in fact historically modern, the long dress is now often seen as the traditional form of Herero dress. Both the older leather dress and the more recent long dress are elaborate items of clothing, the latter involving considerable skill and expense to produce and maintain in good order. A proper long dress is made up of several parts – bodice, arms, skirt, numerous petticoats, optionally an apron or scarf, as well as the headdress – and consists of up to 10 metres (33 ft) of cloth.

While the original fashion for wearing dresses is probably mainly due to Nama influence, specific designs and dress-making skills were introduced by the European missionaries and their wives working in Hereroland. As in the case of the male uniforms of the *Otruppe*, the long dress then became part of the development and transformation of Herero society. In terms of social function, the long dress symbolizes adult female responsibilities, and is an outward sign of the transition from childhood to adulthood. In terms of aesthetics, it is often linked to the centrality of cattle to Herero life. A correctly worn long dress induces in the wearer a slow and majestic gait, while the rounded shape produced by the high waistline and multiple petticoats is reminiscent of the fullness of well-fed cows, as well as of their feminine and life-giving qualities. The most direct resemblance is provided by the headdress. Following older designs of leather caps with three curved 'horns', the two horizontal folds of the modern headdress adopt a bolder, more abstract, yet clear and direct interpretation of cattle horns.

The formation of the *Otruppe* movement can be seen as a pivotal moment in the history of the Herero. Coming after the First World War and the end of German colonial rule, it provided a form of social structure both in addition and as an alternative to family and clan structures; offered help and support for members in need through subscriptions; and, perhaps most importantly, helped to develop a new, rekindled identity for post-war Herero society. For a short time in the 1920s and 1930s, the *Otruppe* assumed a more political role, representing an alternative to official and traditional leadership. However, with the annexation of Namibia by South Africa, and the subsequent introduction of the apartheid system in 1948, there was little room for division, and political activism was directed towards independence, which was eventually achieved in 1990. During the last few decades, new research has revealed a more detailed picture of Herero history (see, for example, page 104), and there has been considerable debate in academia and politics about the Herero genocide and its relation to other colonial wars and to the Nazi genocides of the mid-twentieth century.

Portraits

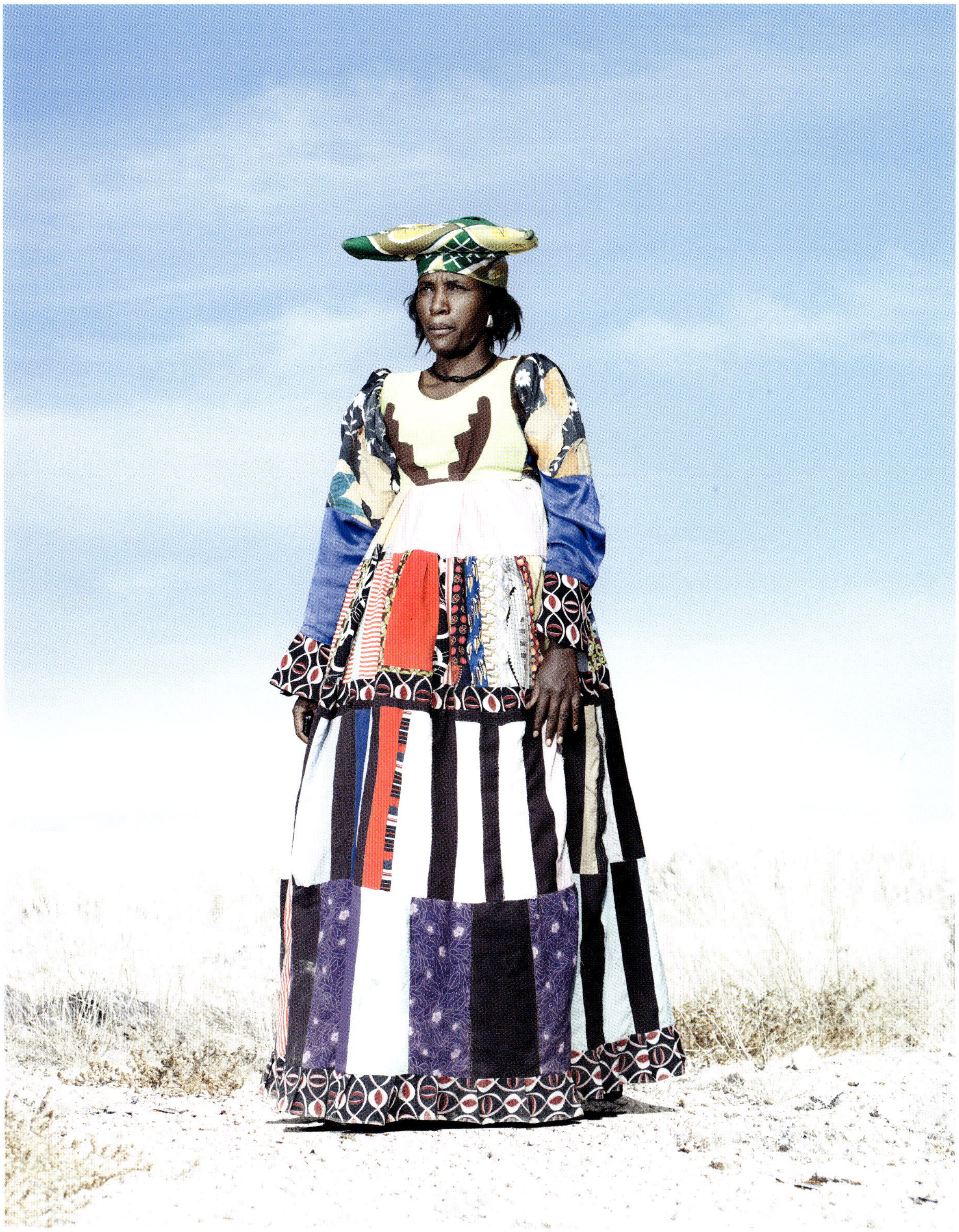

A Herero woman wearing a patchwork dress.
Often worn as daywear or for work,
such dresses usually consist of offcuts
from other outfits.

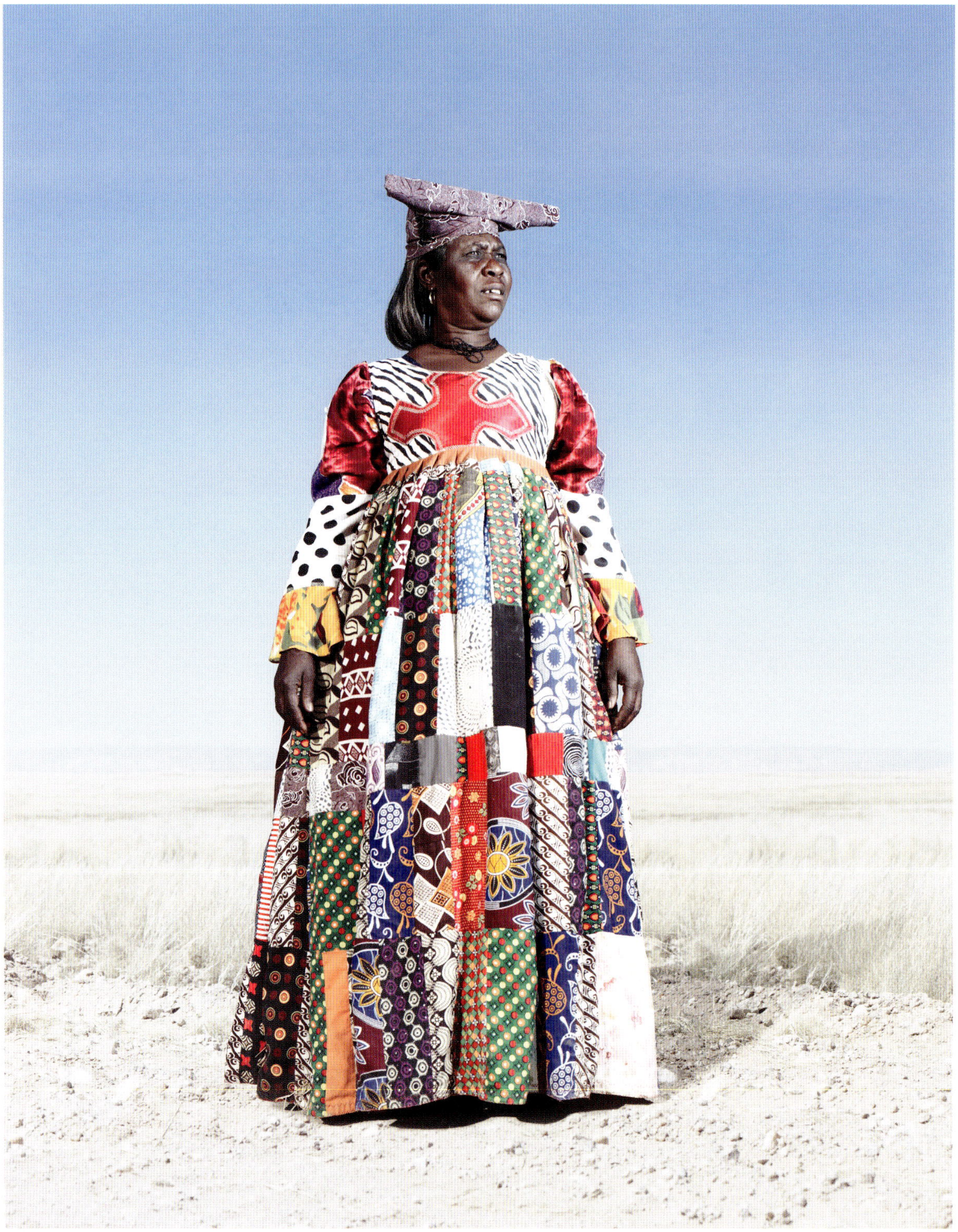

Designed to represent a pair of horns, the
distinctive headdress worn by Herero women,
as seen here, symbolizes the importance
of cattle to the Herero way of life.

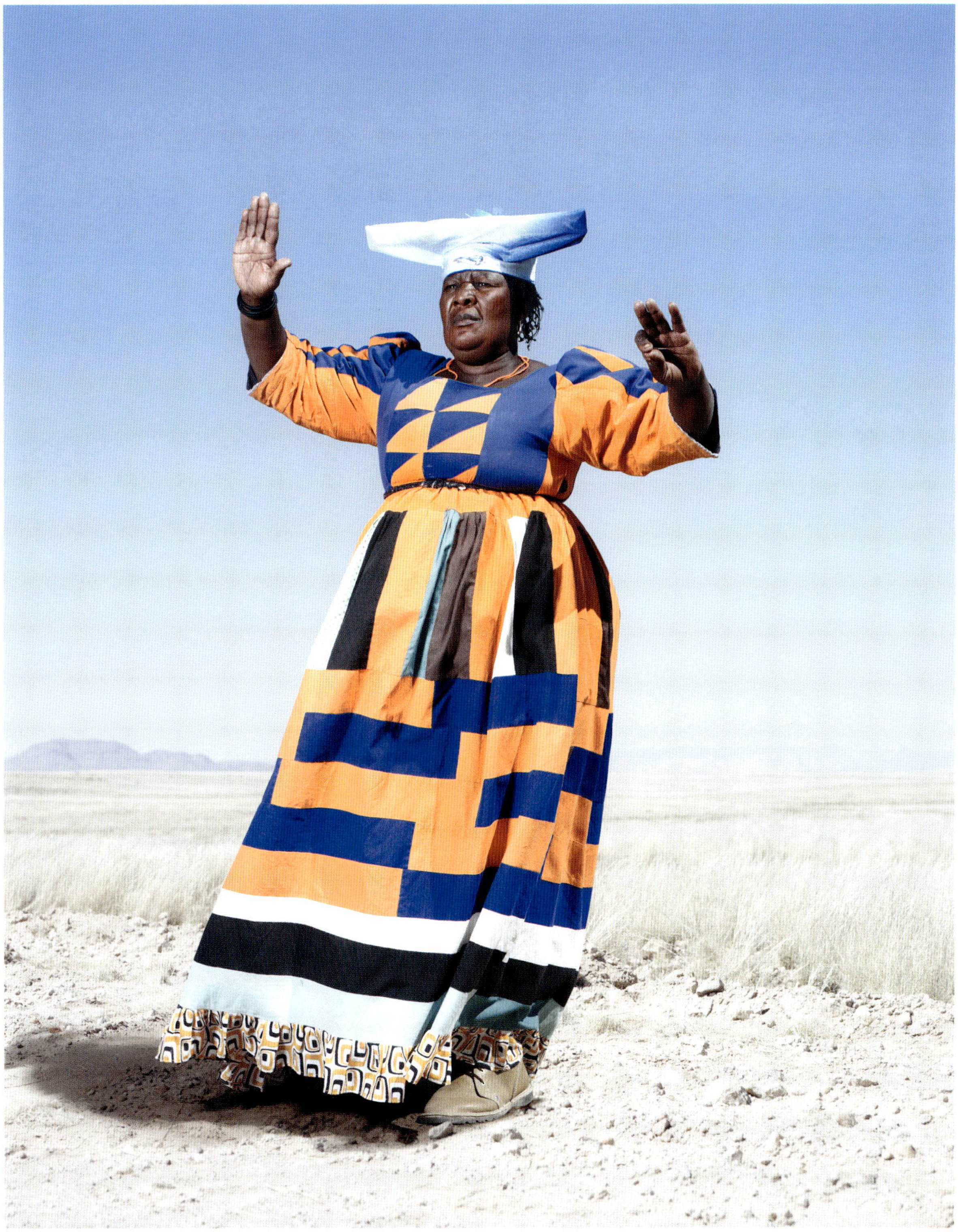

A Herero woman demonstrating the cow dance. Although relatively little is known about the exact origins or meaning of the dance, it is yet another indication of the centrality of cattle to Herero society.

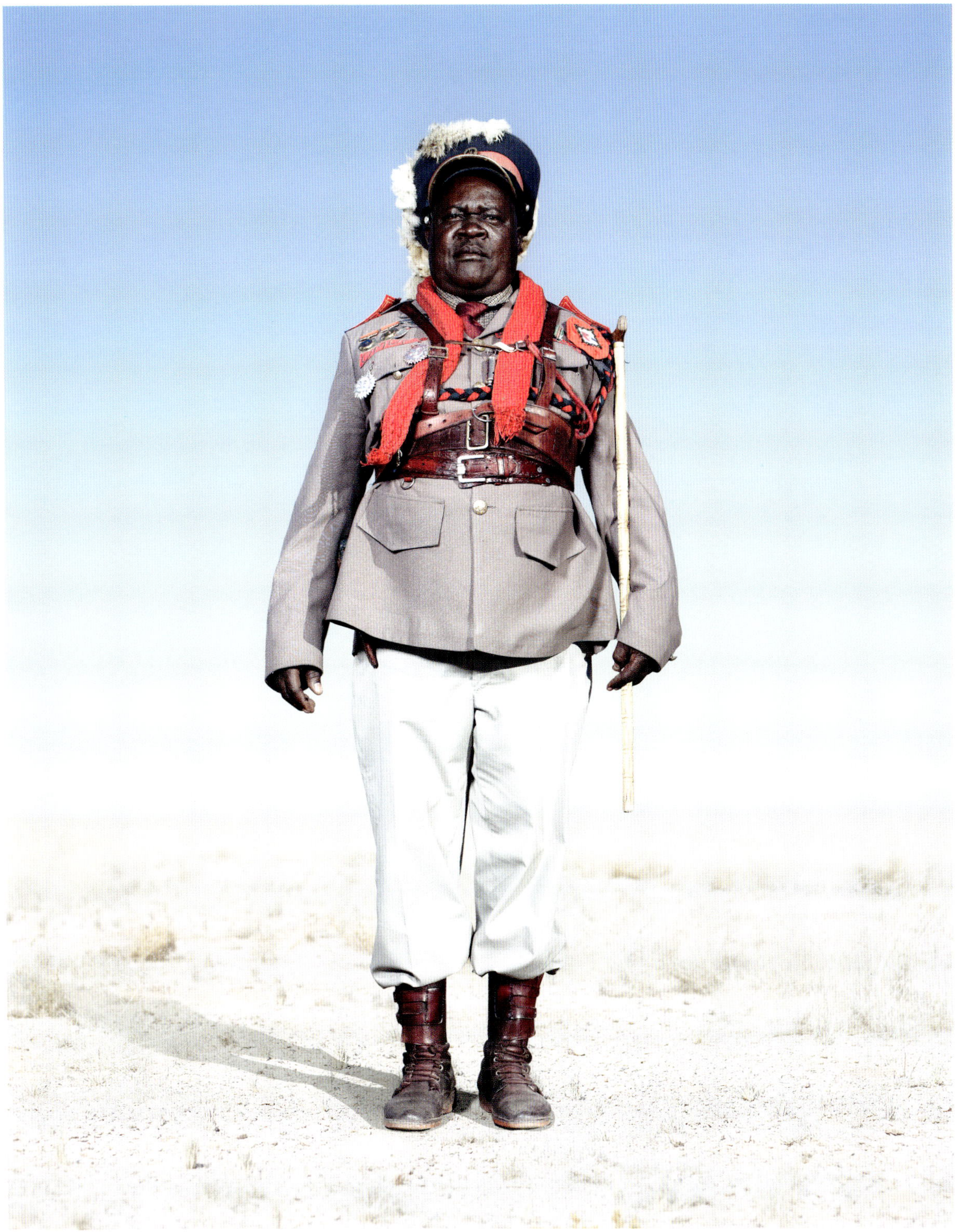

An *Otruppe* group leader. The wearing of fur on hats is a traditional sign of bravery. In this case, the fur is that of a jackal.

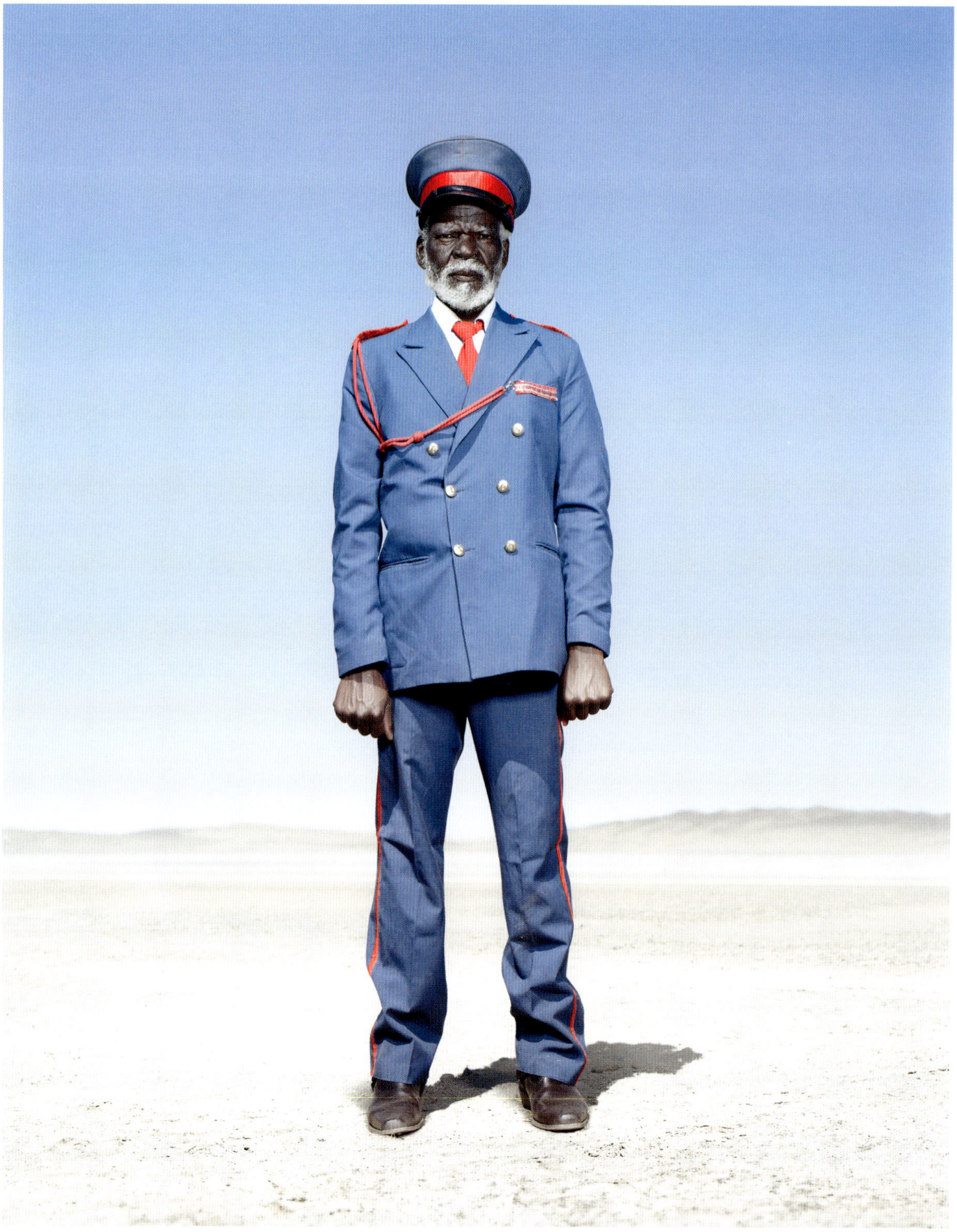

An *Otruppe* soldier in blue uniform. The Herero first began wearing military uniforms in the second half of the nineteenth century, when they were given as gifts to chiefs by traders from the Cape.

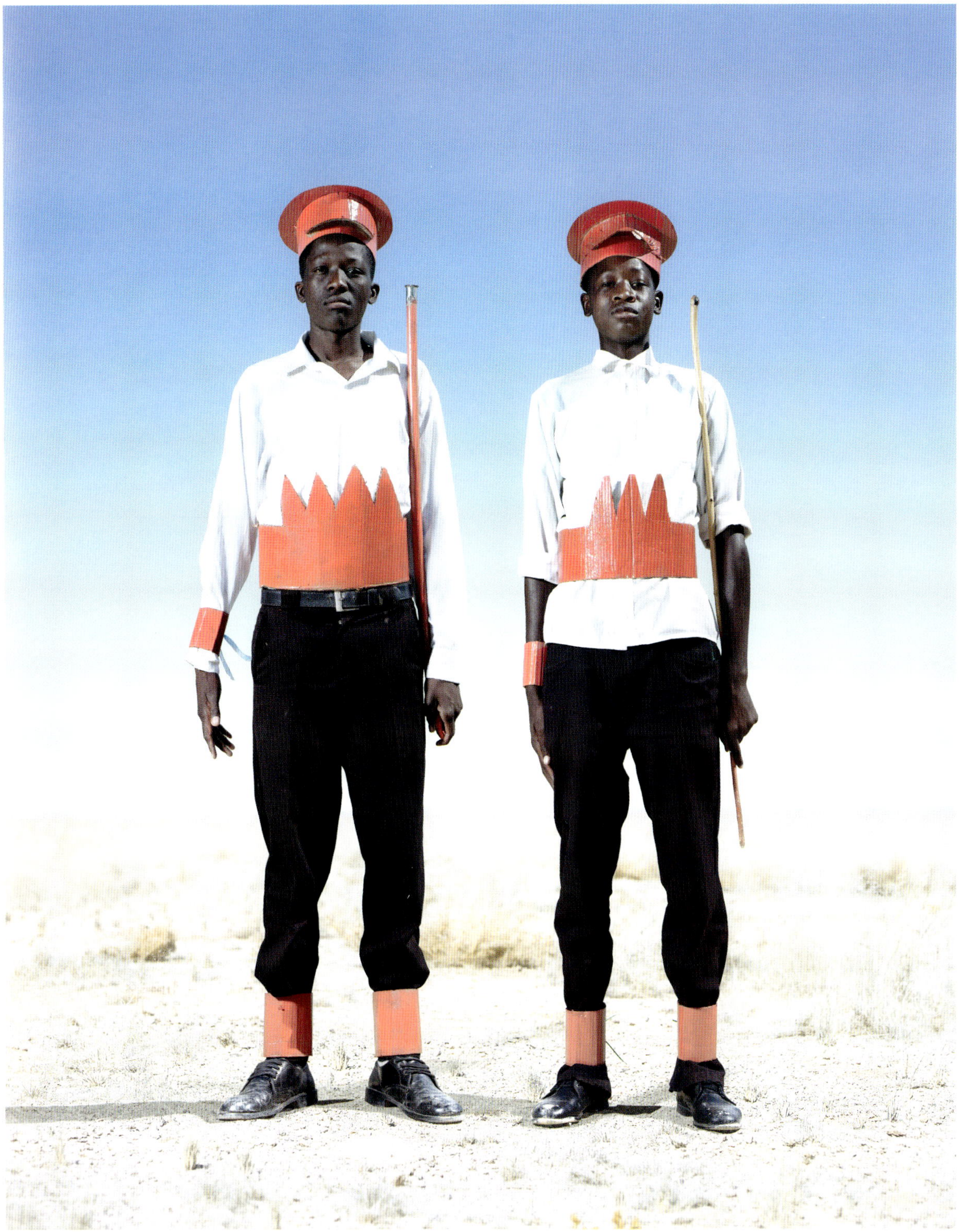

Two *Otruppe* cadets. The cardboard elements of their uniforms – the caps, sashes, and wrist and ankle bands – were made by the cadets themselves, for public marching demonstrations.

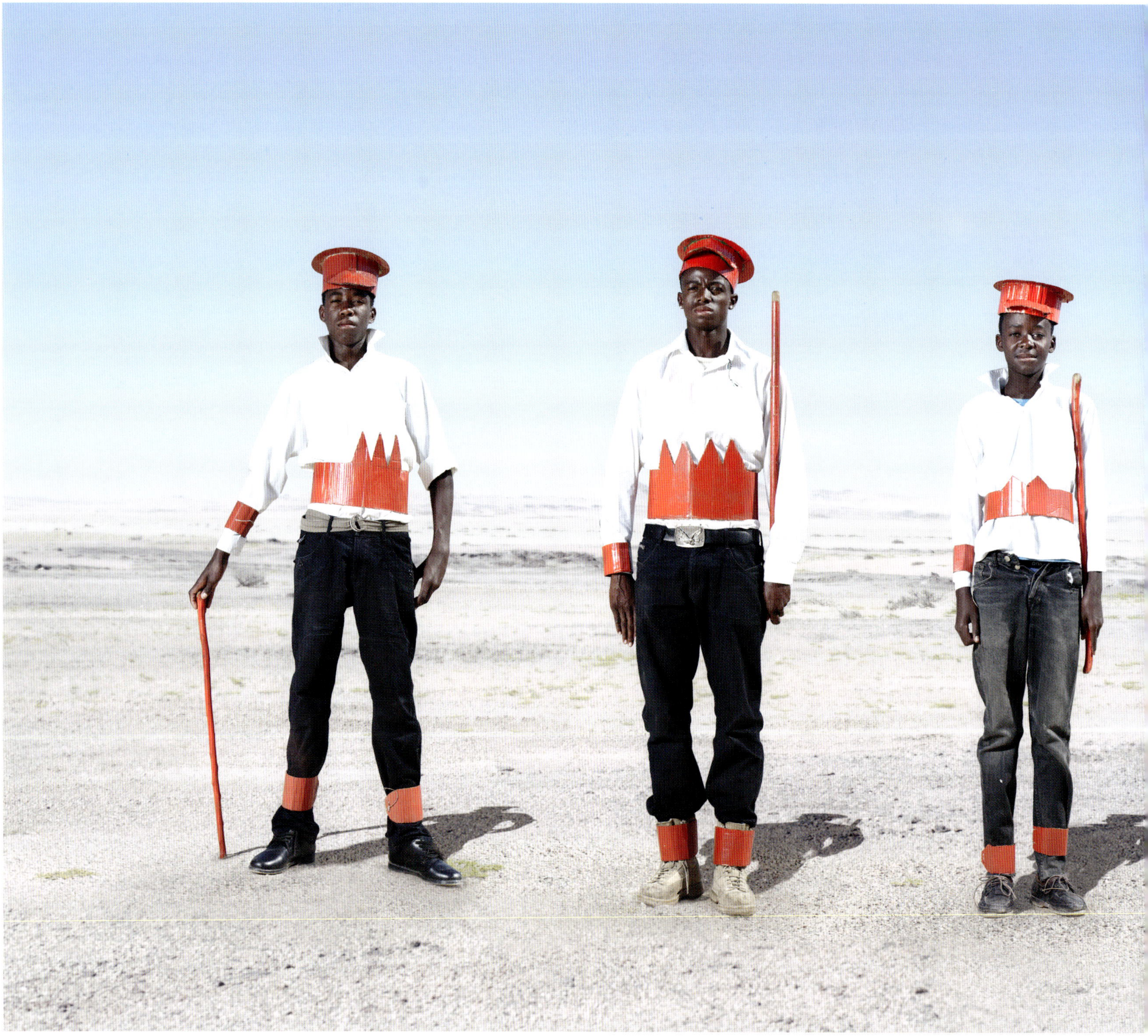

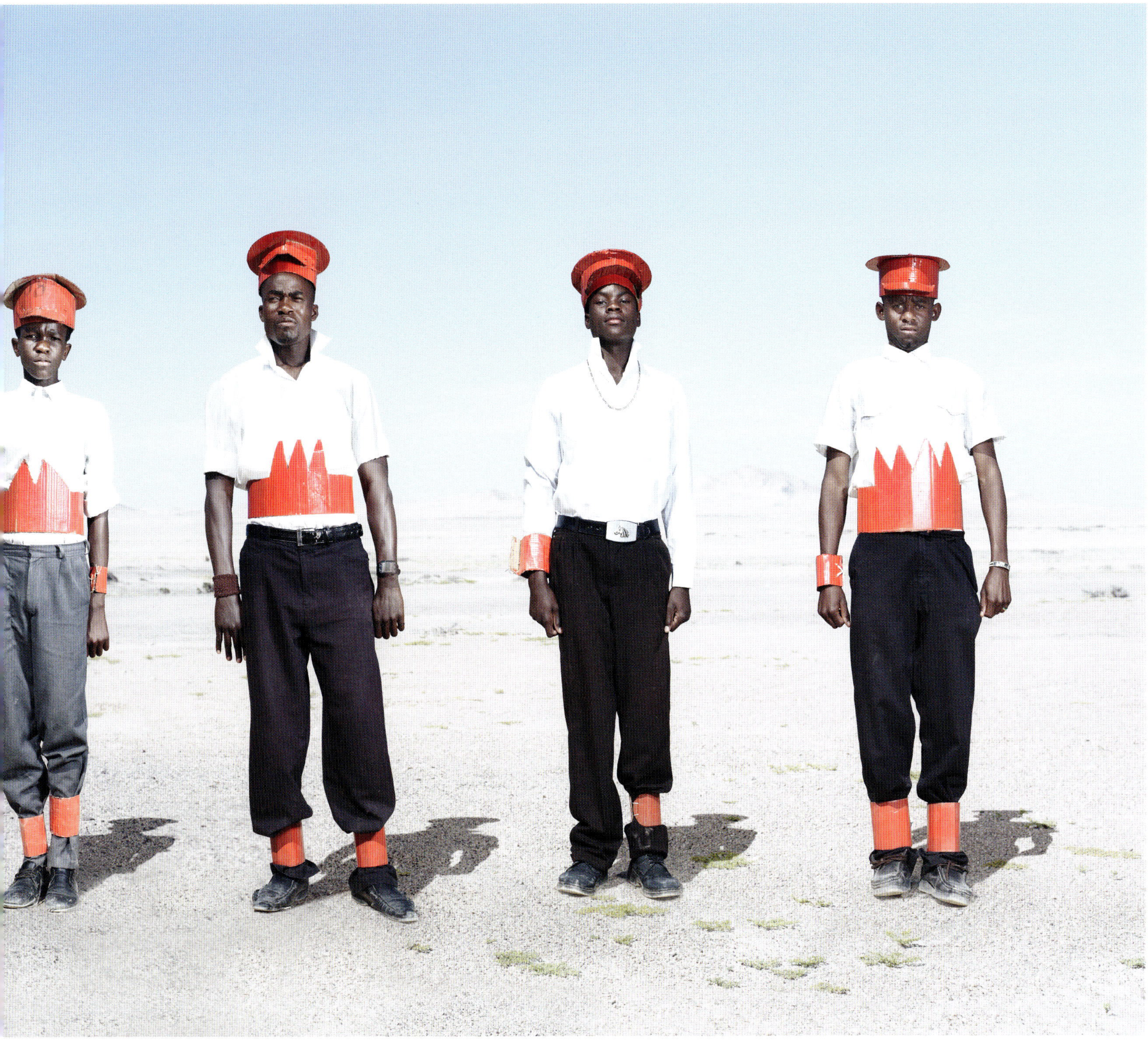

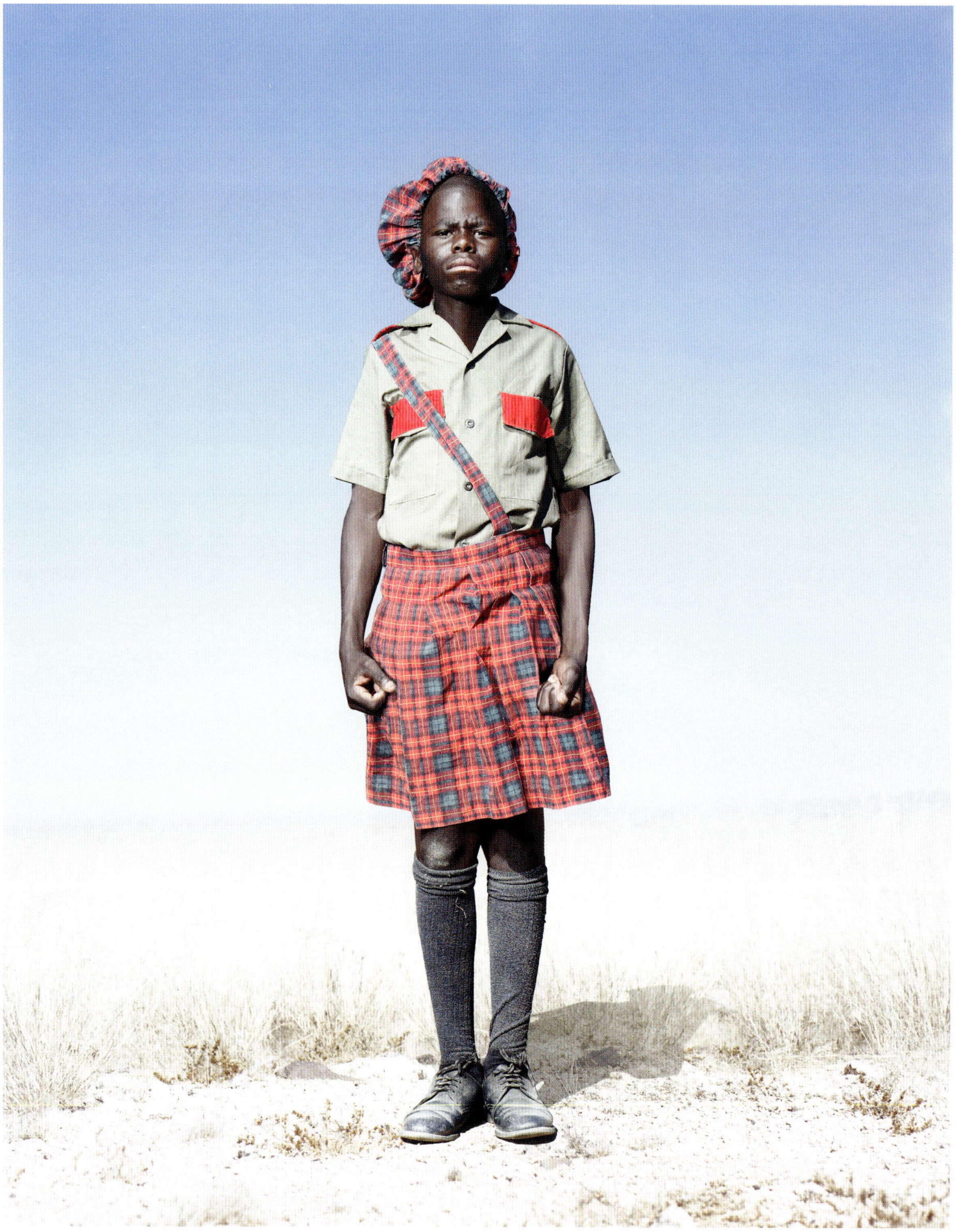

The military attire of the *Otruppe* has been influenced by a variety of sources. Here (above and opposite), two cadets wear the uniform of an *Otruppe* division that has chosen to dress in the manner of Scottish warriors.

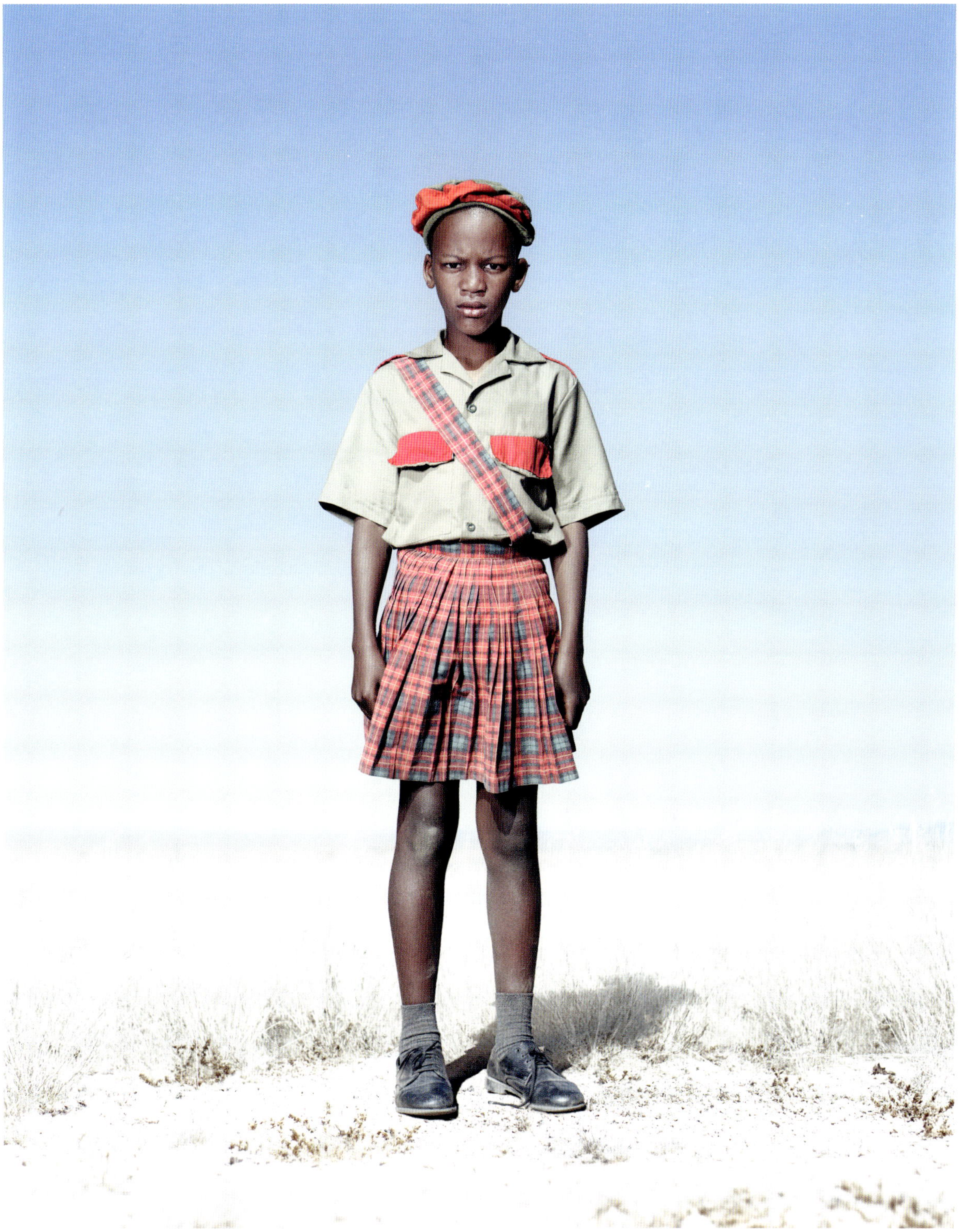

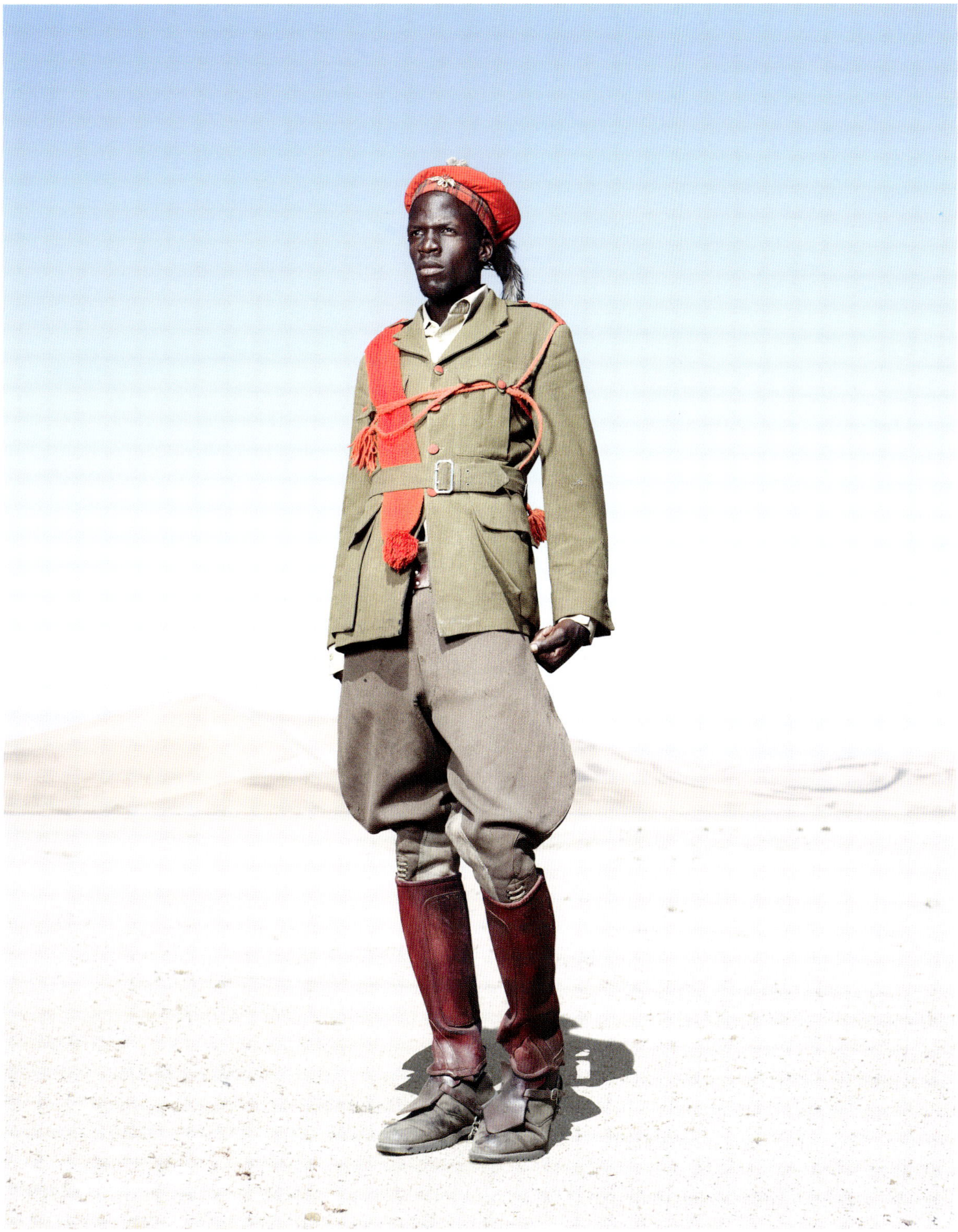

An *Otruppe* cavalryman. His red beret and sash identify him as a member of the *Otjiserandu* section of the *Otruppe*.

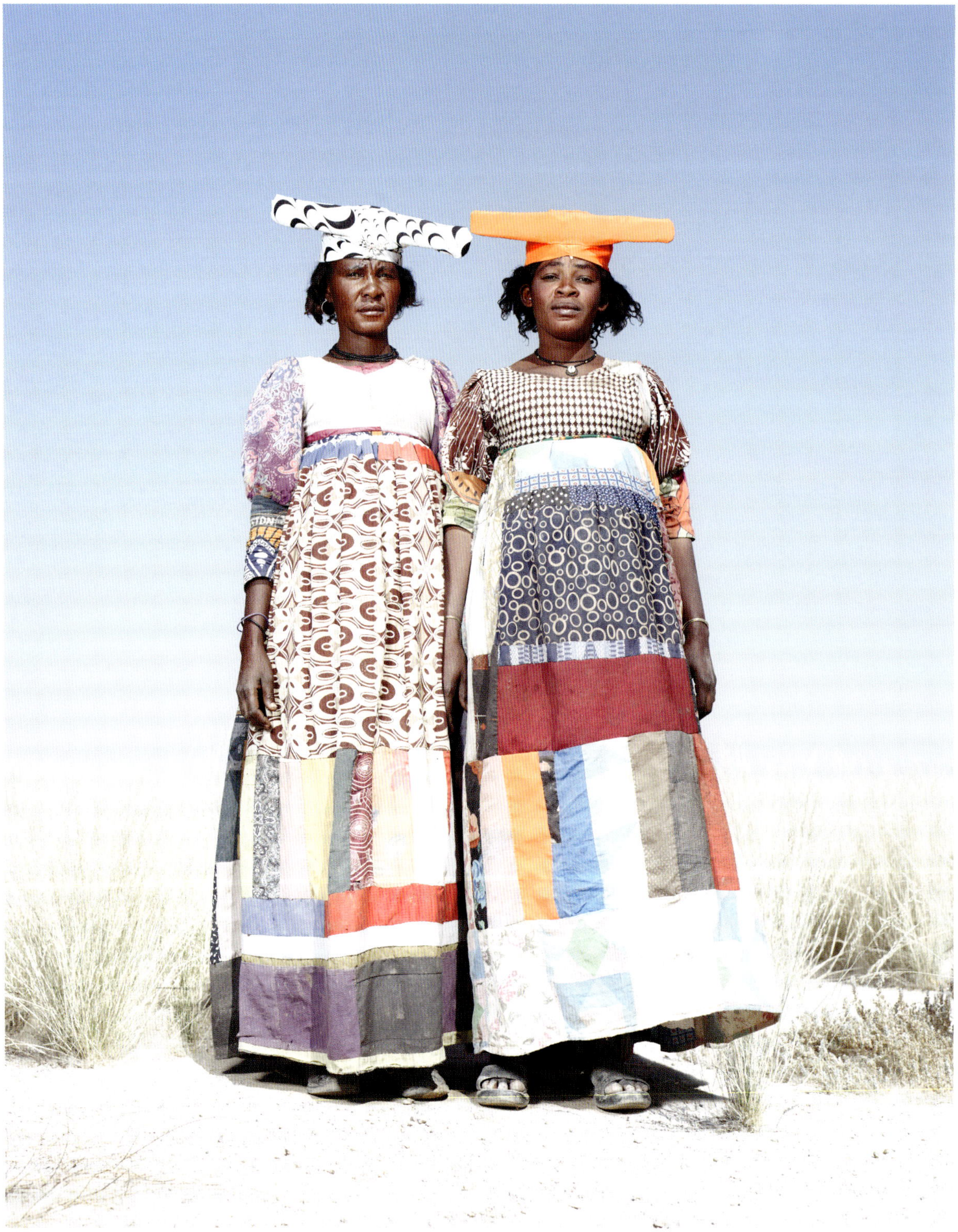

Patchwork dresses, such as those worn by these Herero women (above and opposite), feature a variety of designs, including bold geometric patterns.

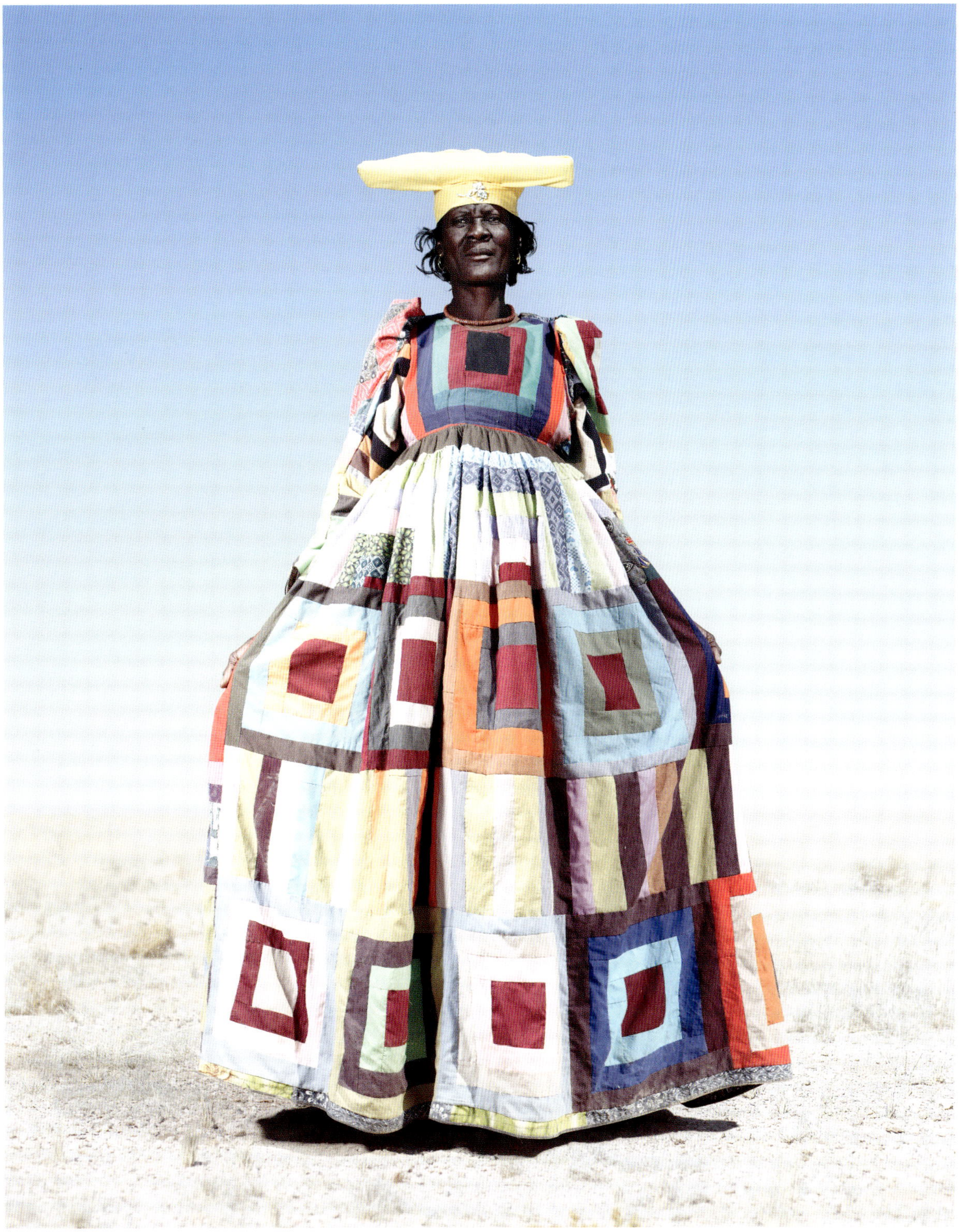

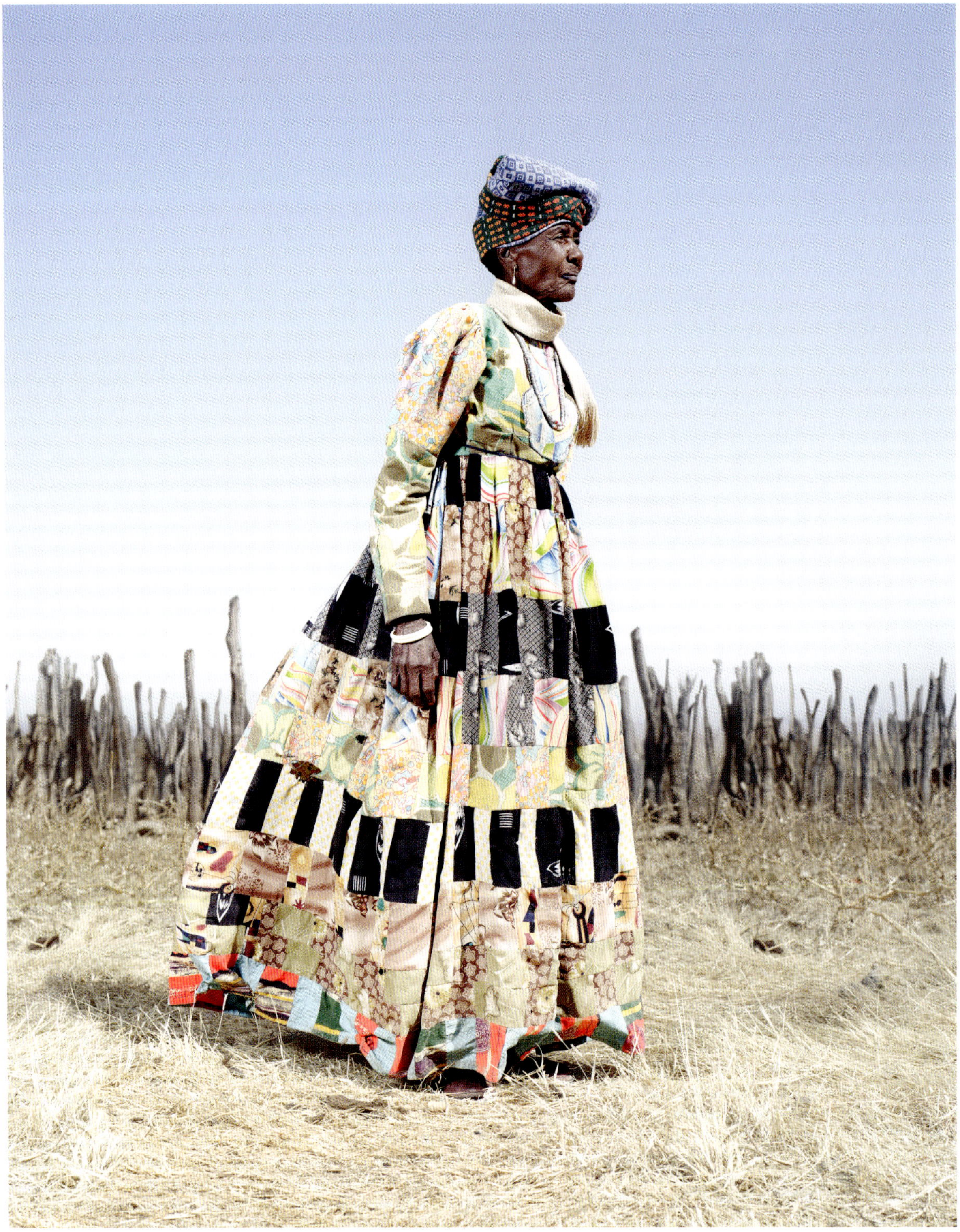

A Herero woman in front of a *kraal*, a roughly circular enclosure for cattle or other livestock.

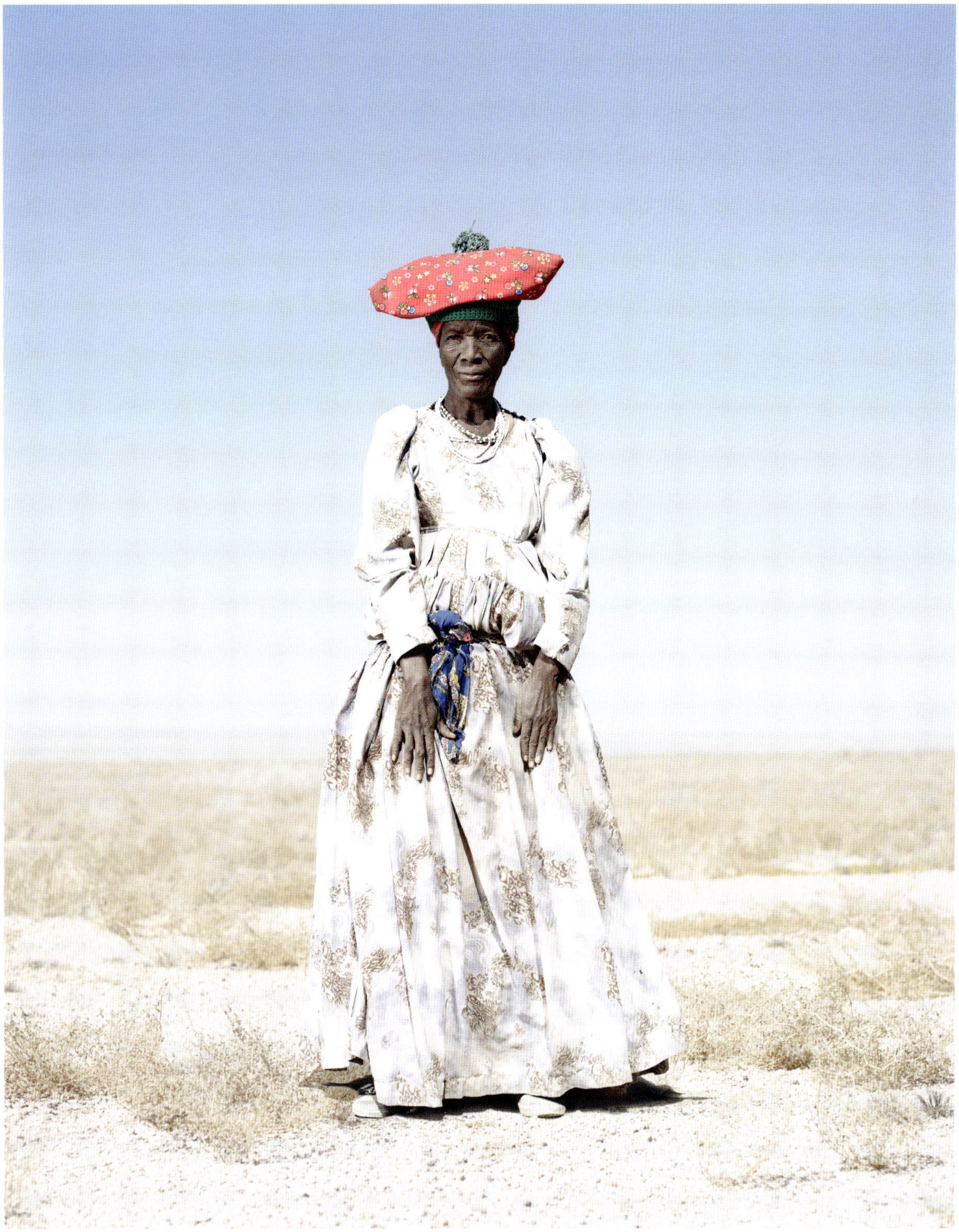

A Herero woman in a patterned long dress. Victorian-style dresses were introduced to the Herero in the mid-nineteenth century by, among others, the wives of German missionaries. Emma Hahn, for example, who was of English descent, ran sewing classes for Herero women from 1846 until at least the 1860s.

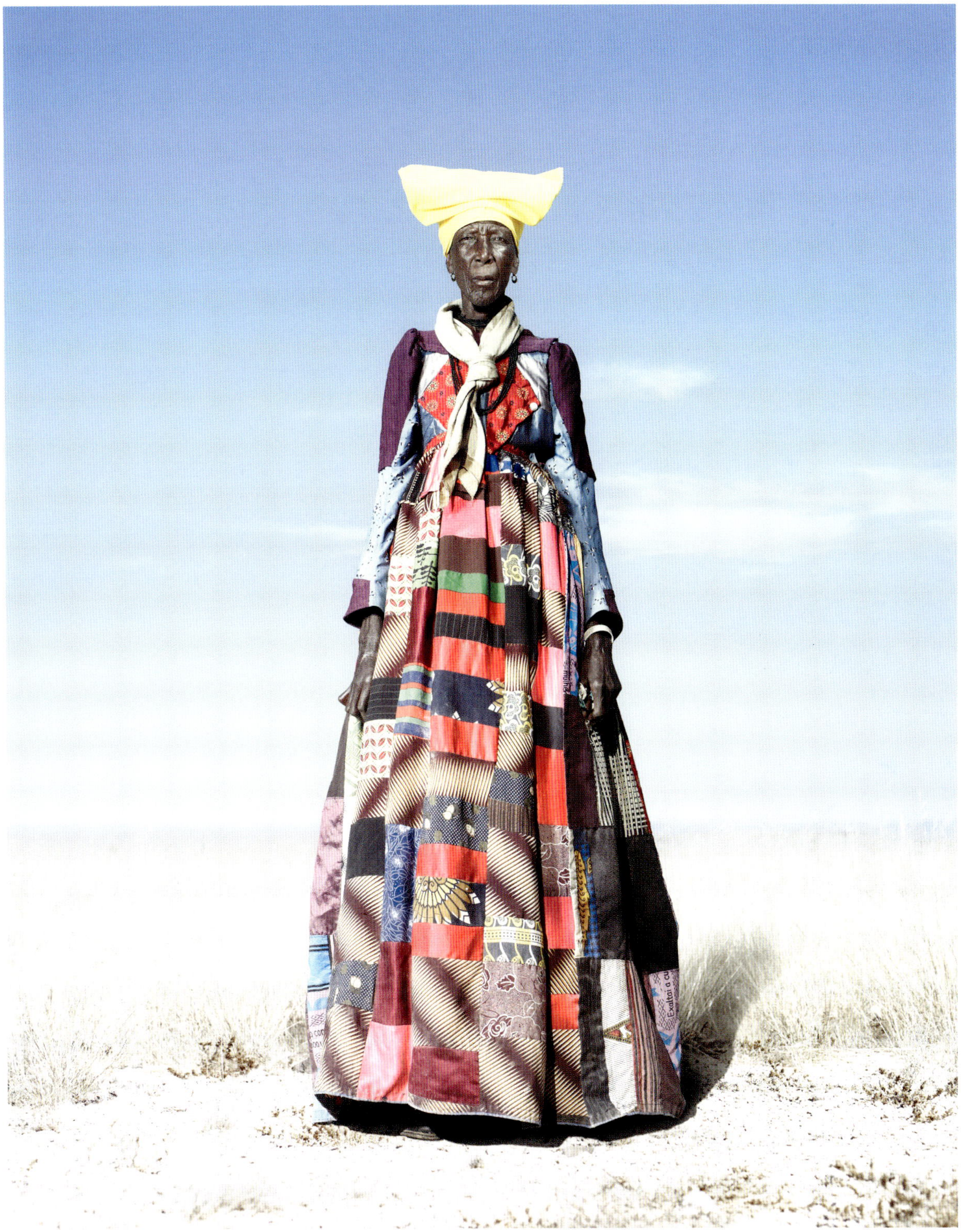

An elderly Herero woman in patchwork dress
and pale scarf. As Herero women get older, the 'horns'
of their headdresses get smaller. According to some
accounts, this is to symbolize their loss of fertility.

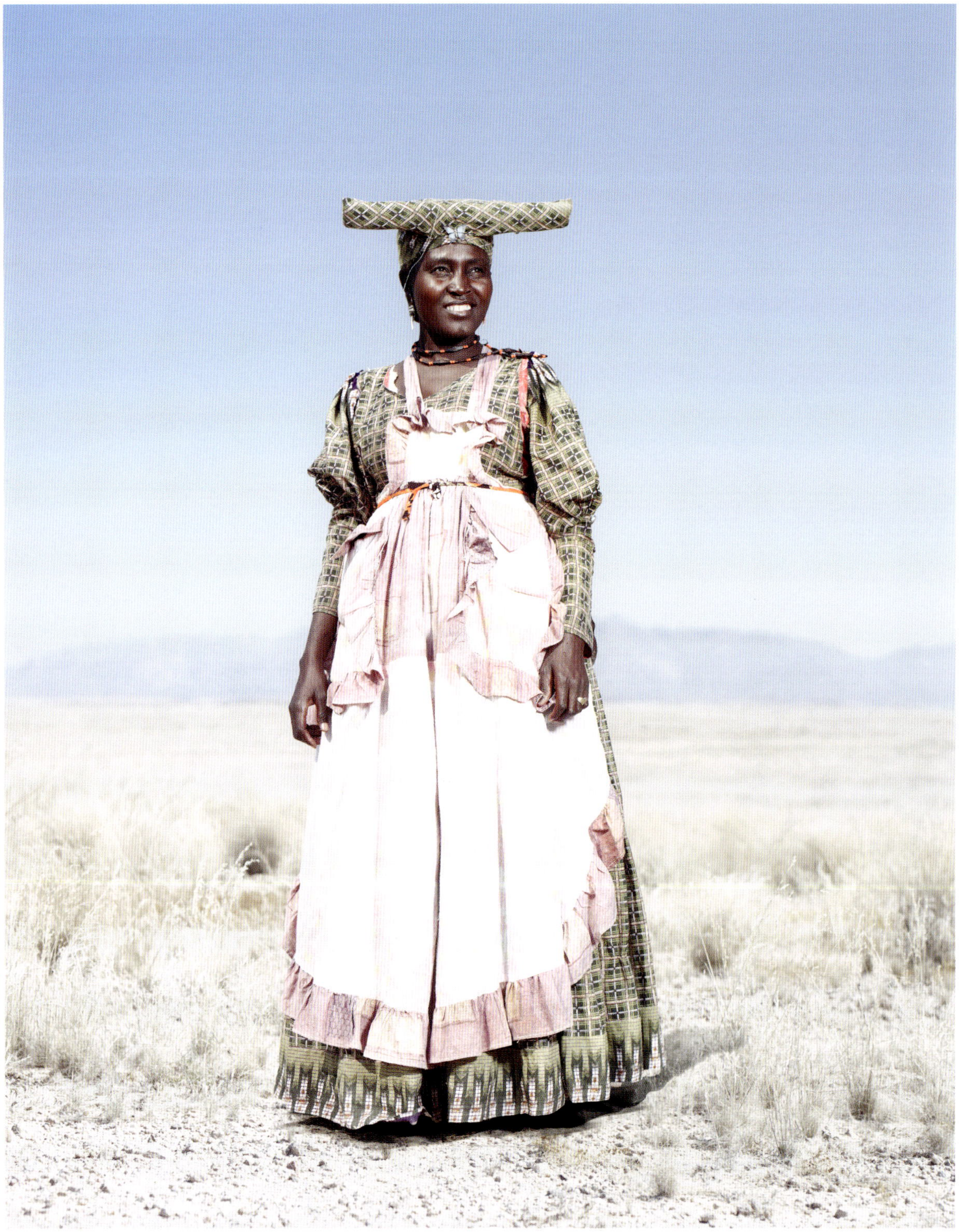

A Herero woman in long dress and apron.

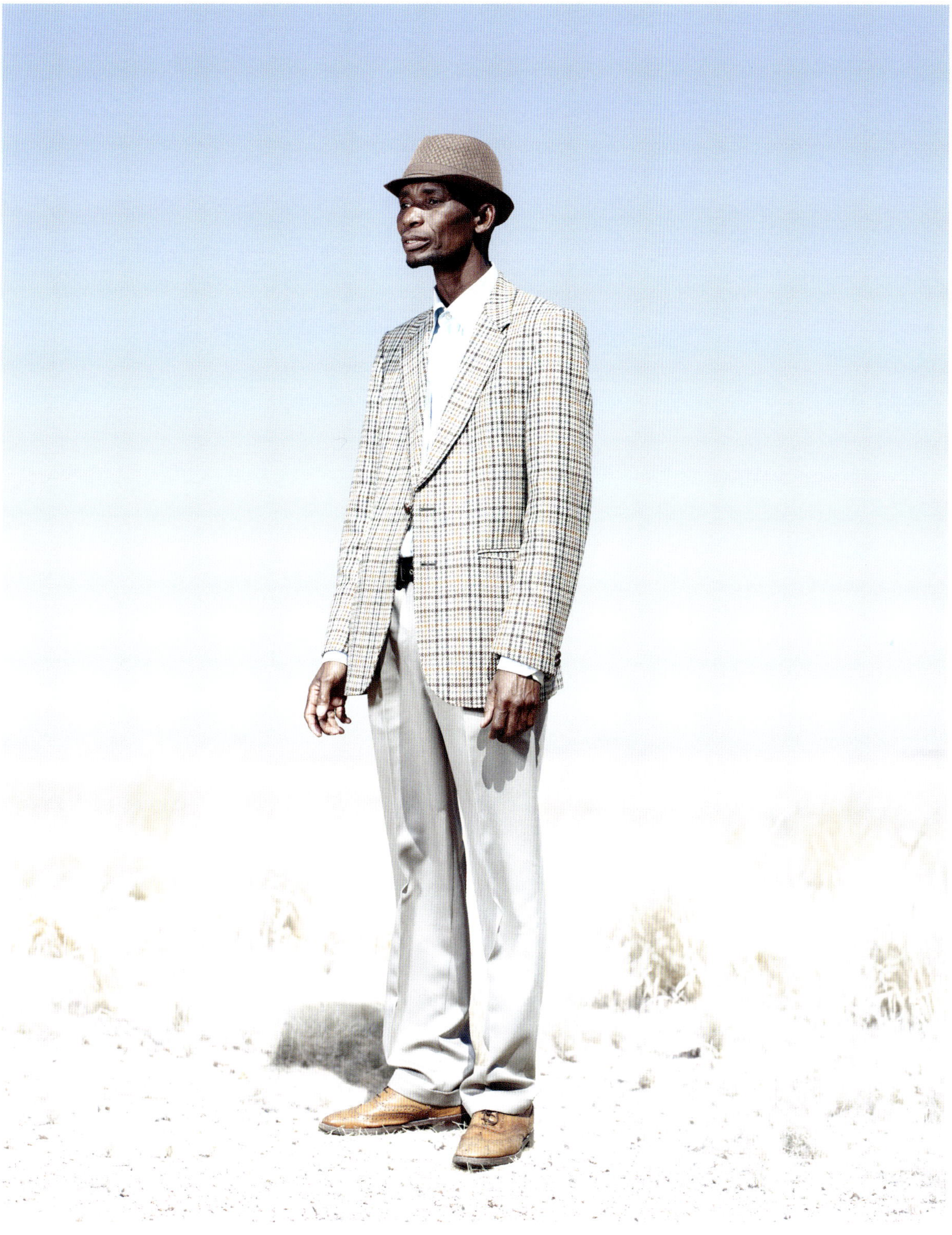

A Herero man in check jacket and trilby. The tradition among Herero men of wearing such formal attire began in the second half of the nineteenth century, following the arrival in Namibia of migrants from the Cape.

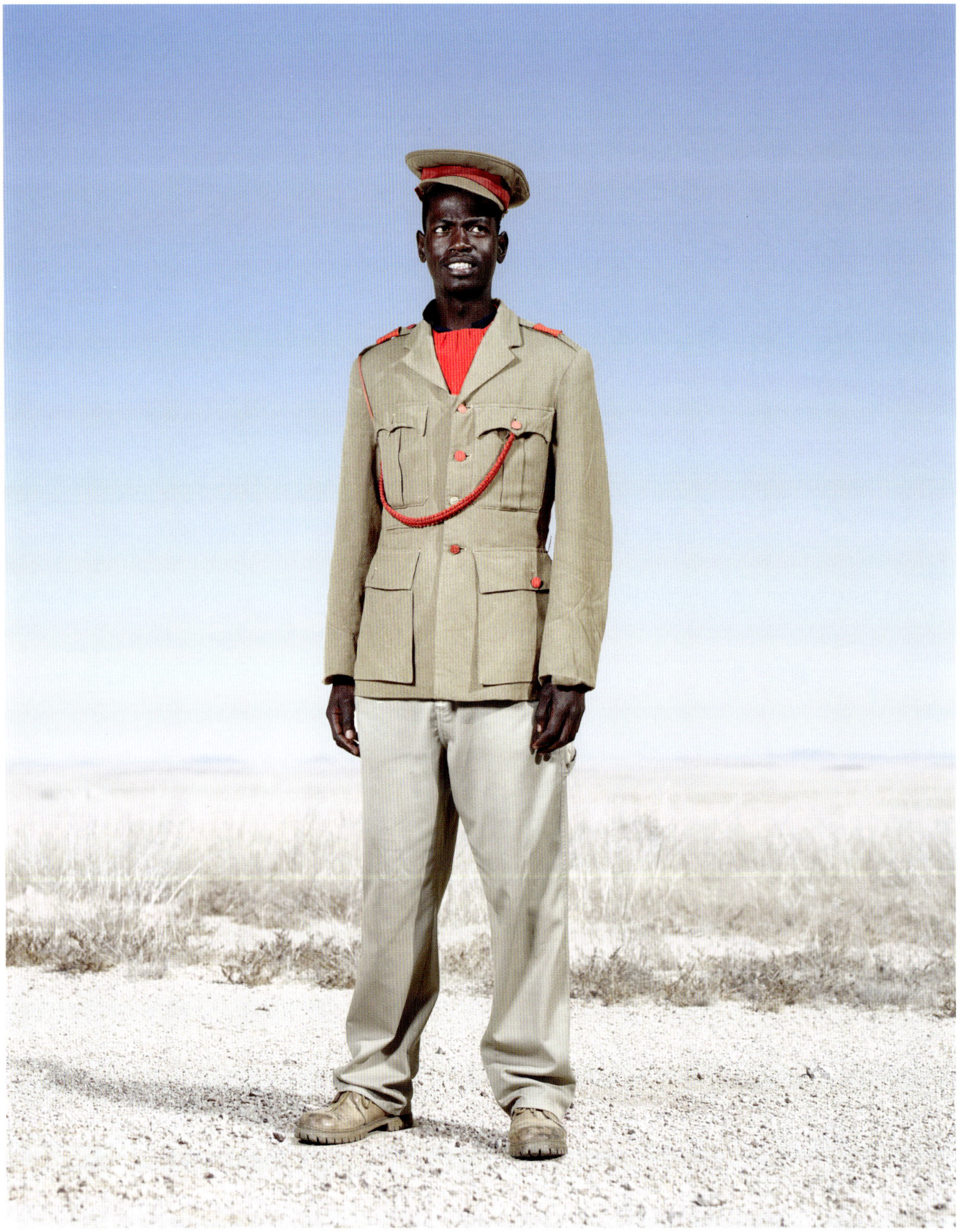

Two *Otruppe* soldiers (above and opposite) from the *Otjiserandu* section.

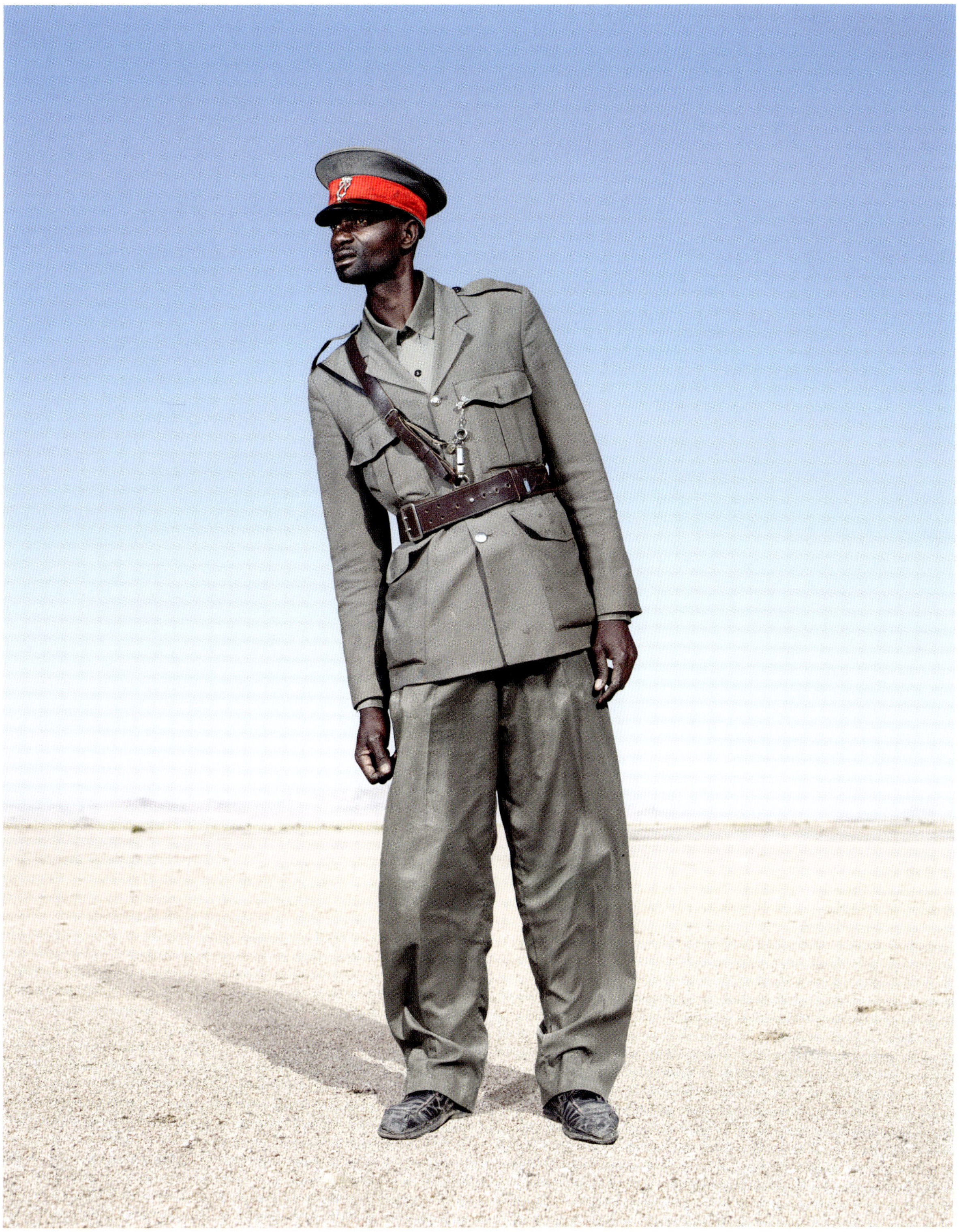

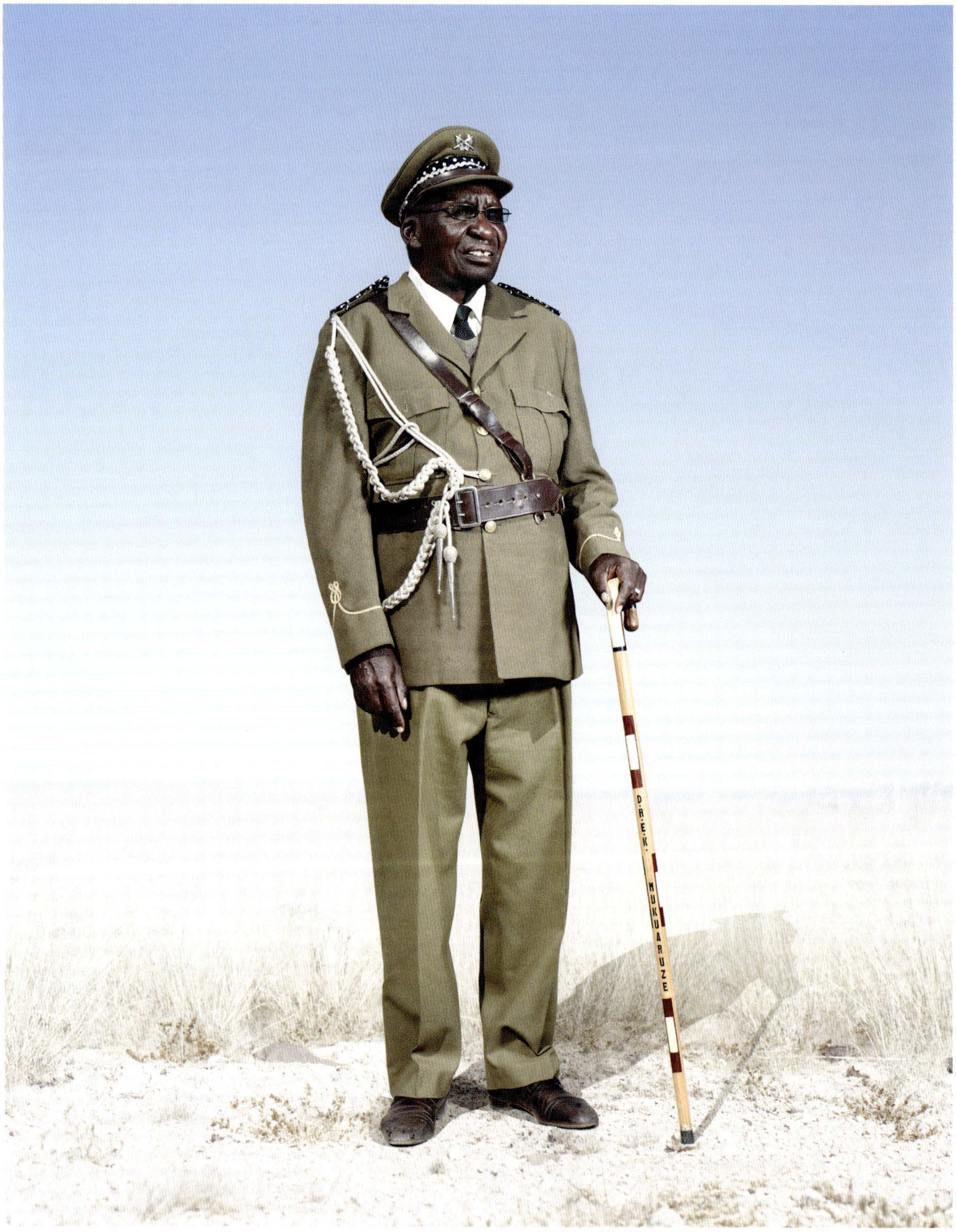

A senior *Otruppe* soldier. The pattern on his headband and epaulettes (white dots on a black background) identifies him as a member of the *Otjizemba* section.

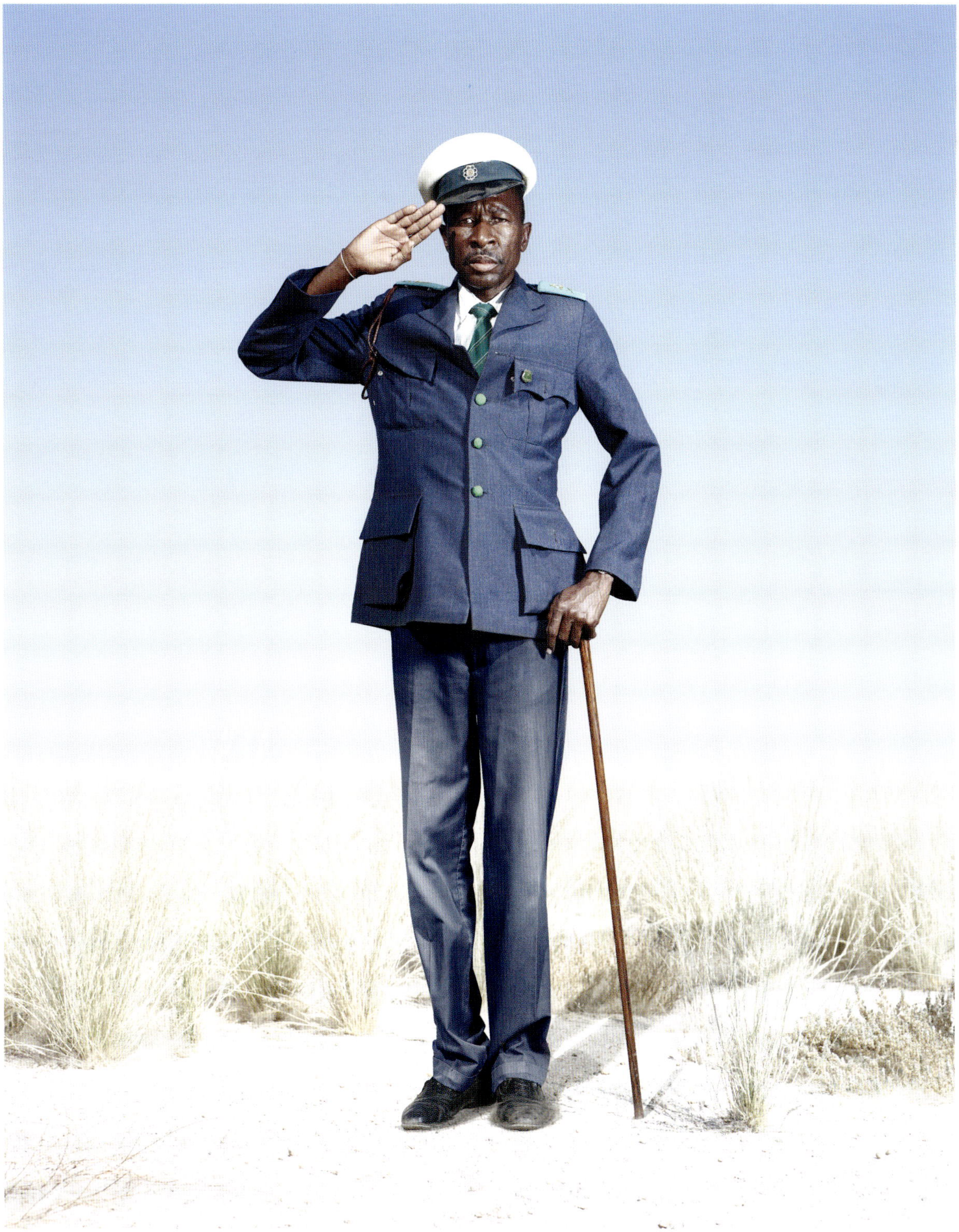

A member of the *Otjigrine* section of the *Otruppe*. The movement's various uniforms have evolved over the years, and often bear little resemblance to those first introduced to the Herero in the mid-1800s.

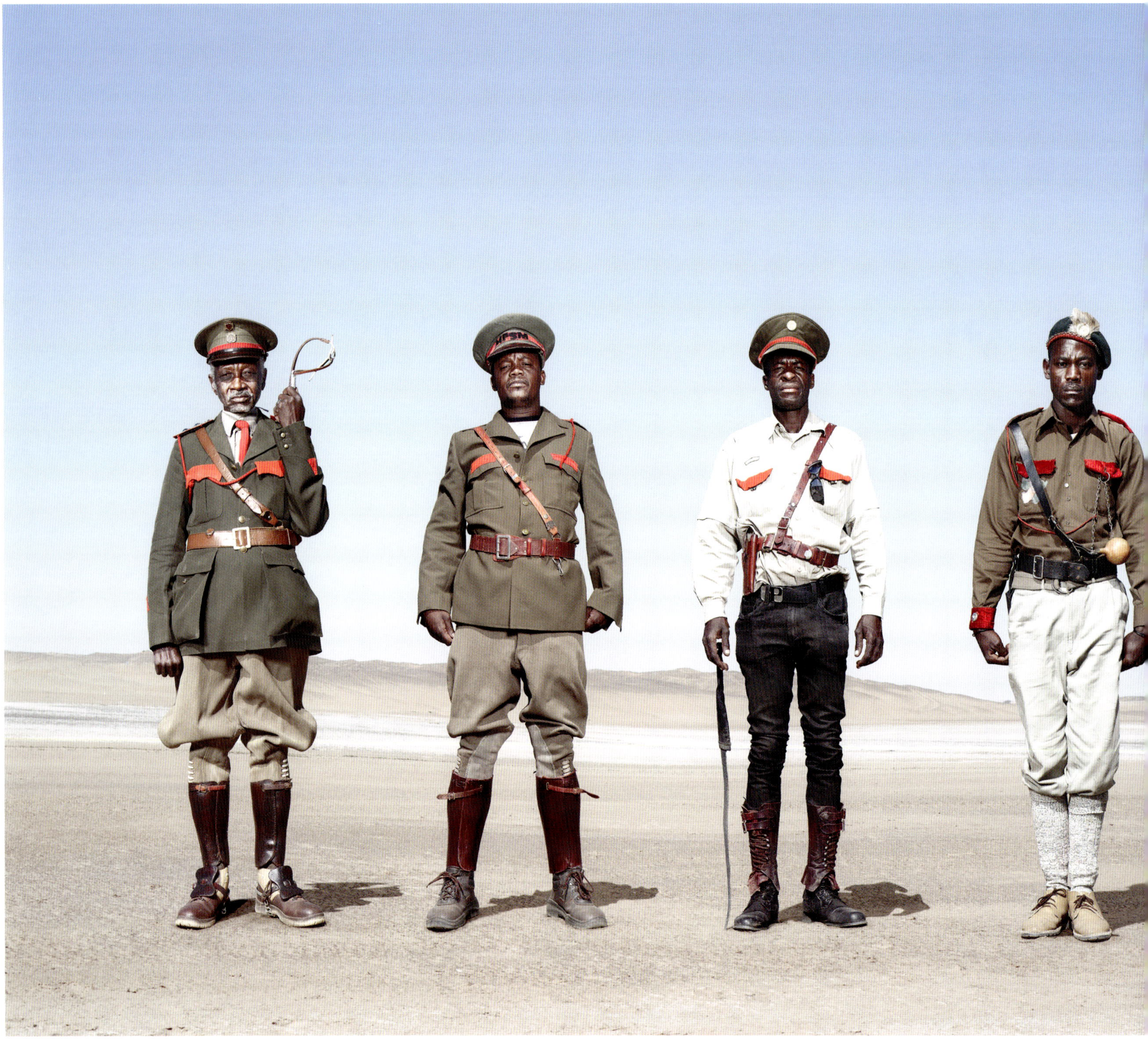

A mix of *Otruppe* soldiers and cavalrymen –
all members of the *Otjiserandu* section –
stand to attention.

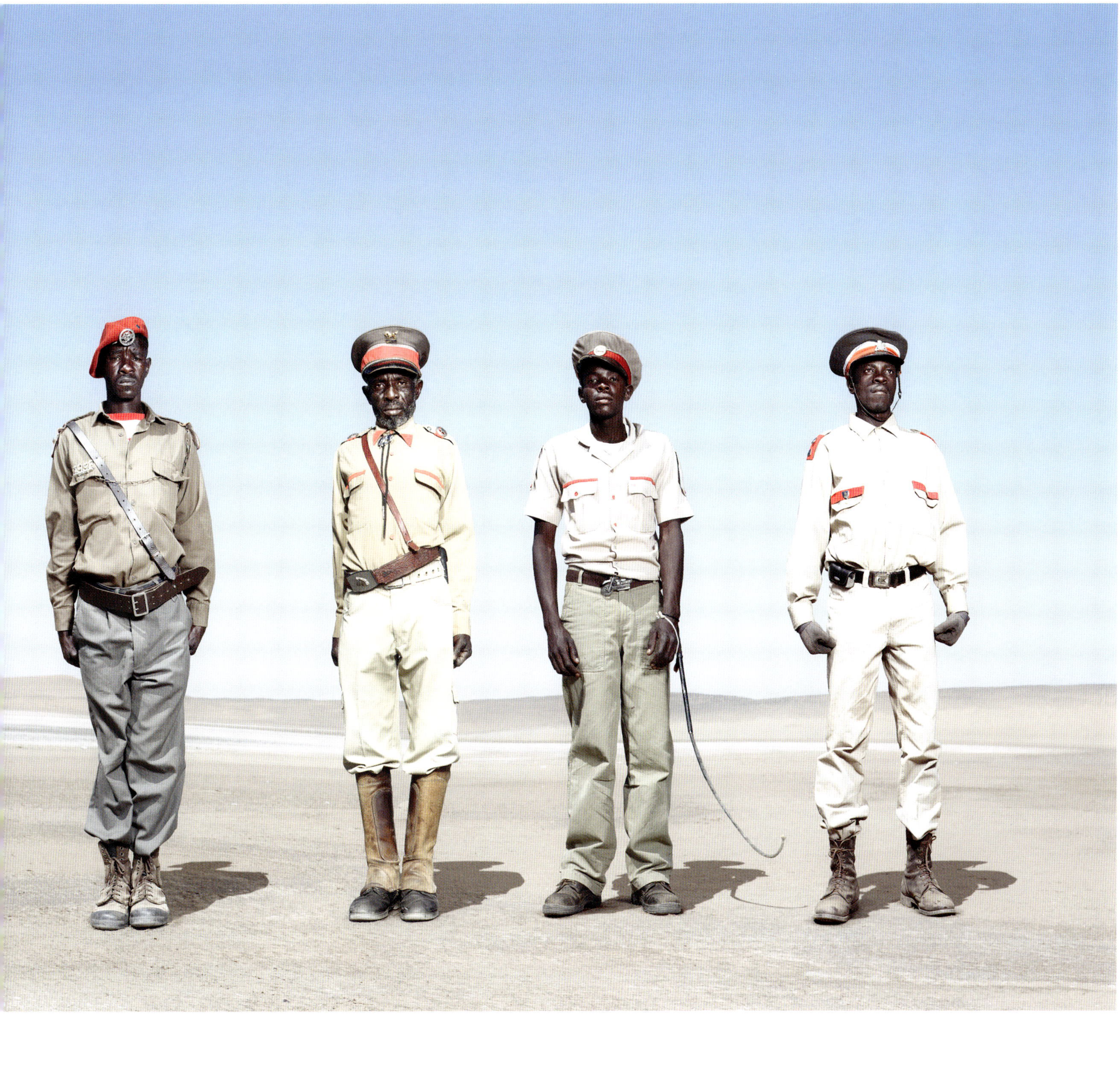

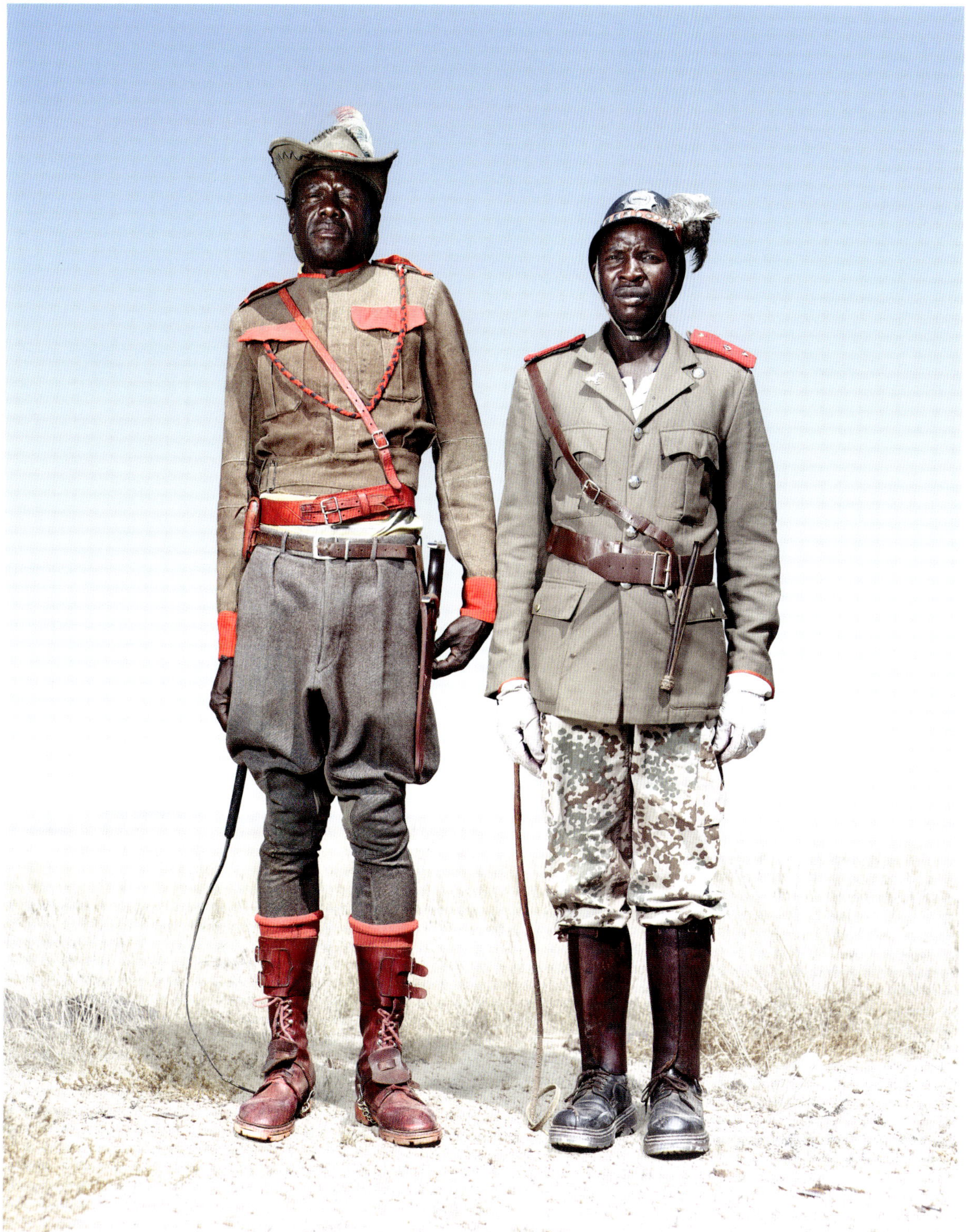

Both skilled riders, these *Otruppe* cavalrymen had ridden for two days to reach a meeting. Their uniforms demonstrate the variety of styles adopted by the *Otruppe*; the man on the right, for example, is wearing a British policeman's helmet.

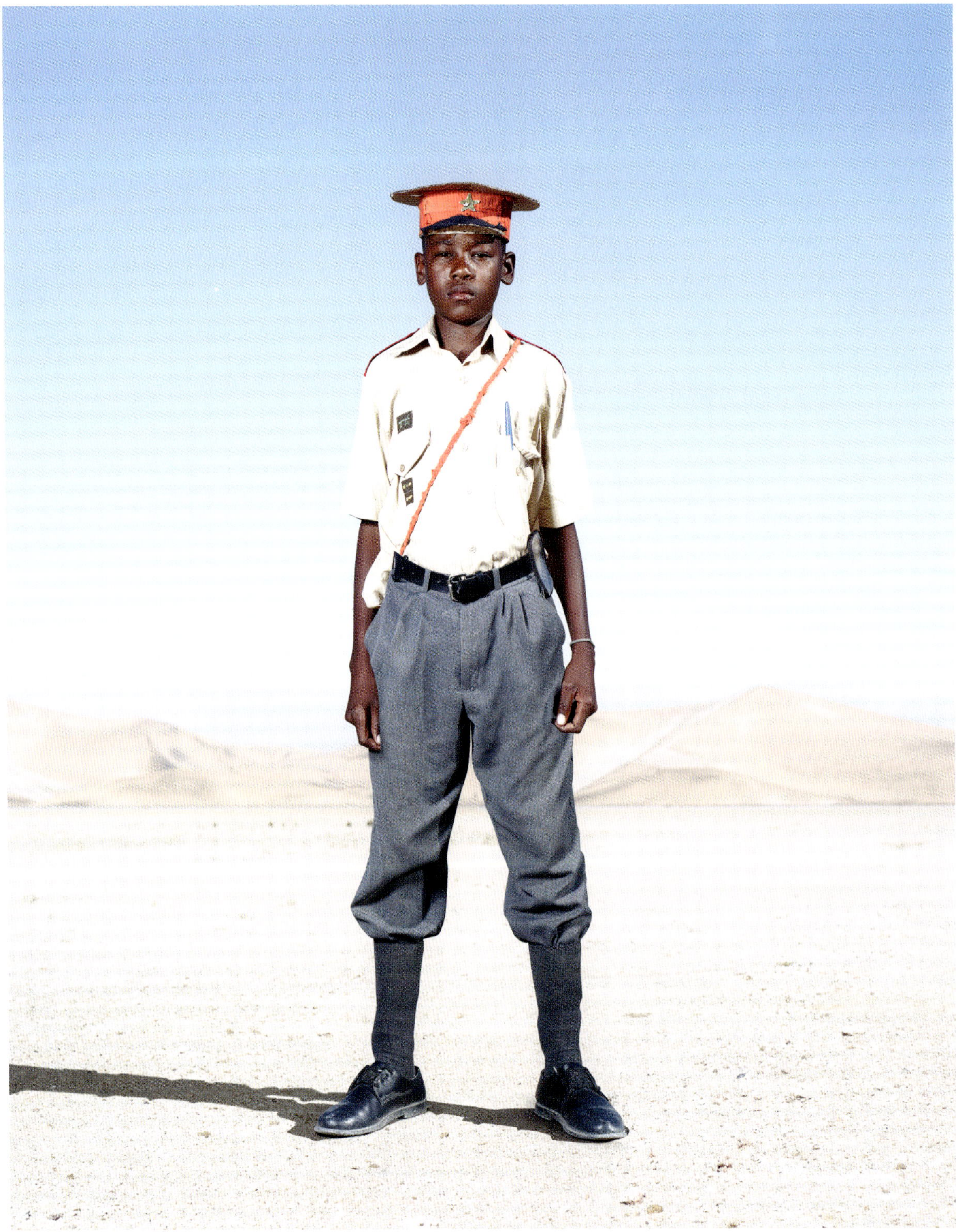

As in the case of these cadets (above and opposite), many members of the *Otruppe* join up while at school.

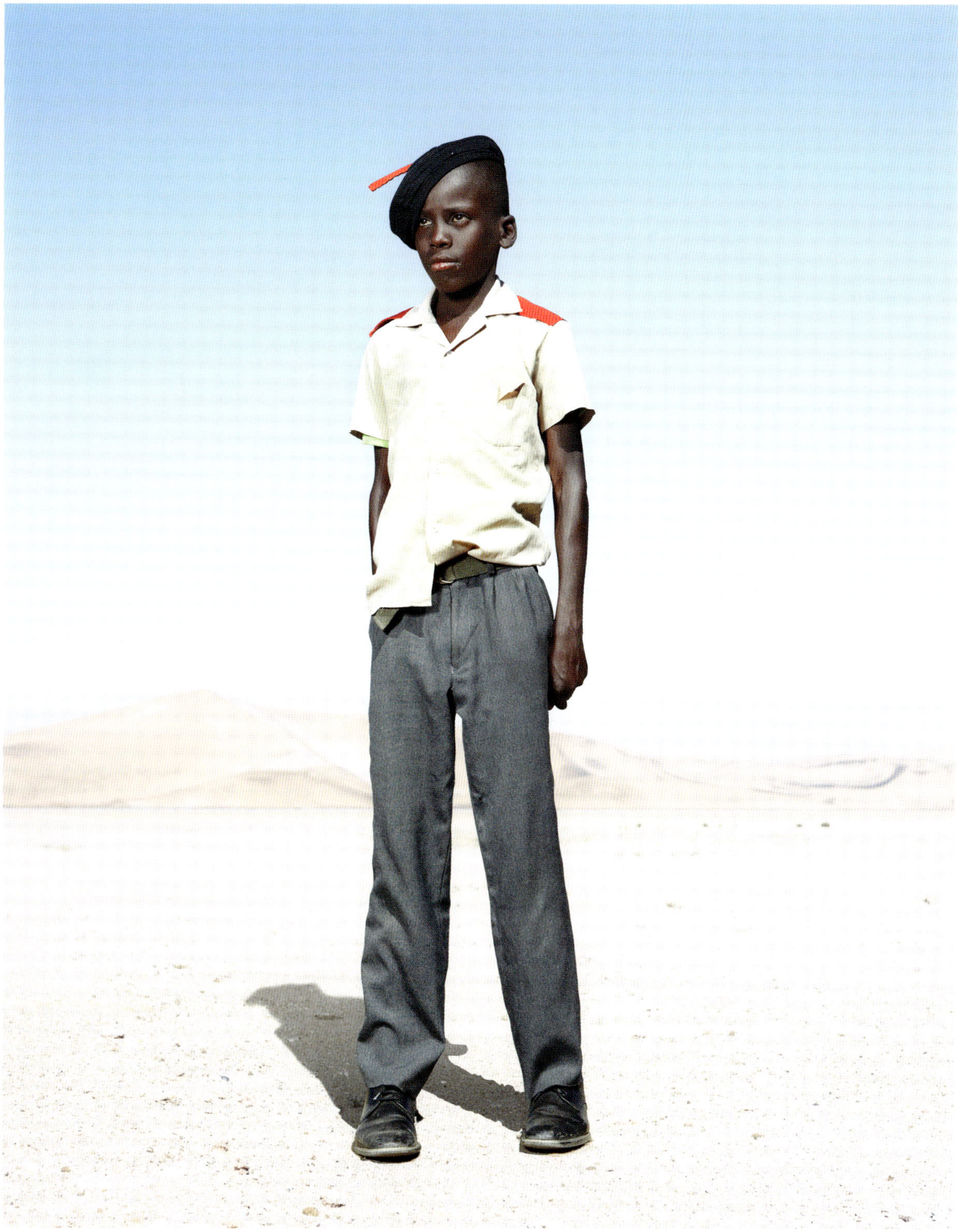

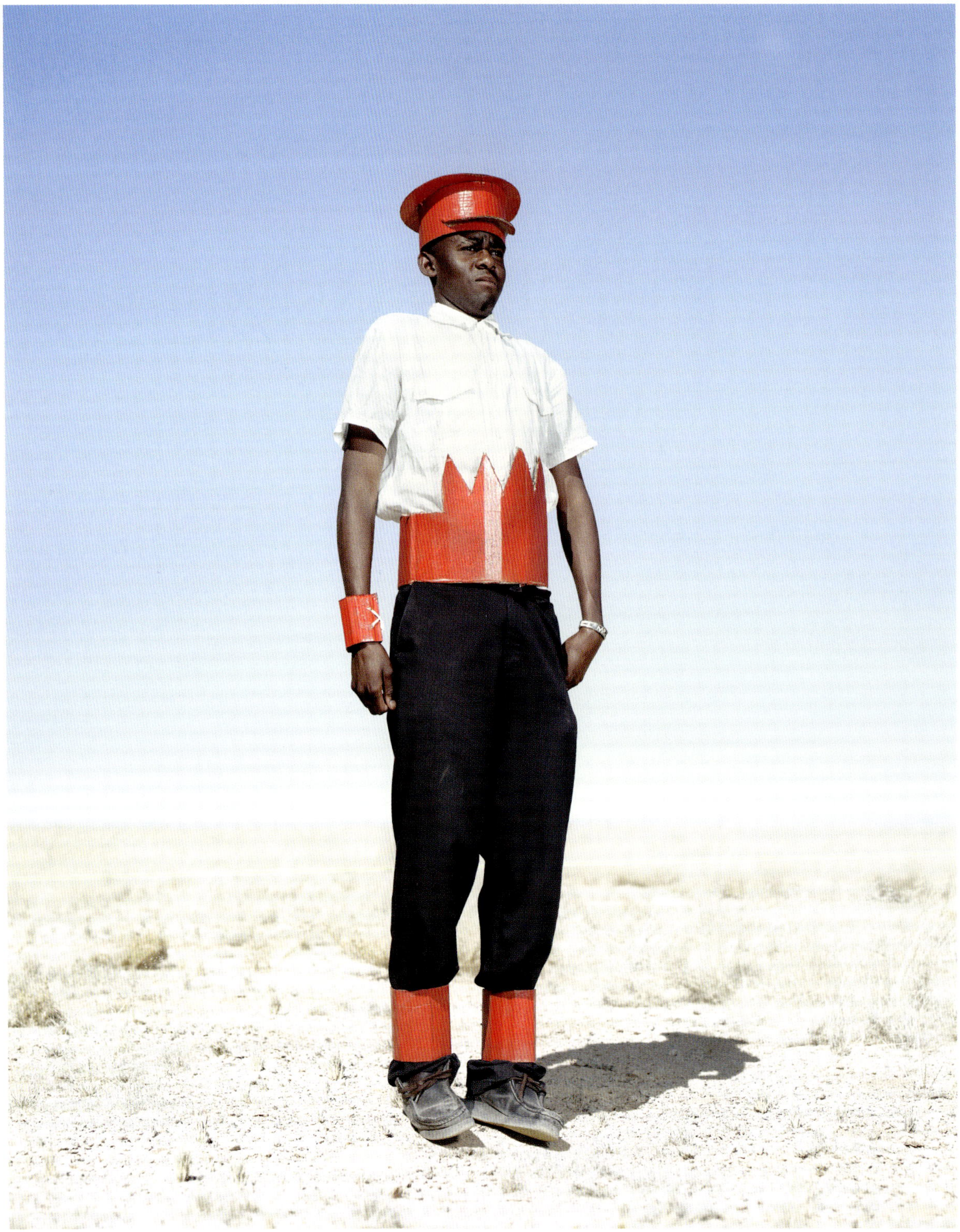

Otruppe cadets (above and opposite) proudly display their partly home-made uniforms (see page 27).

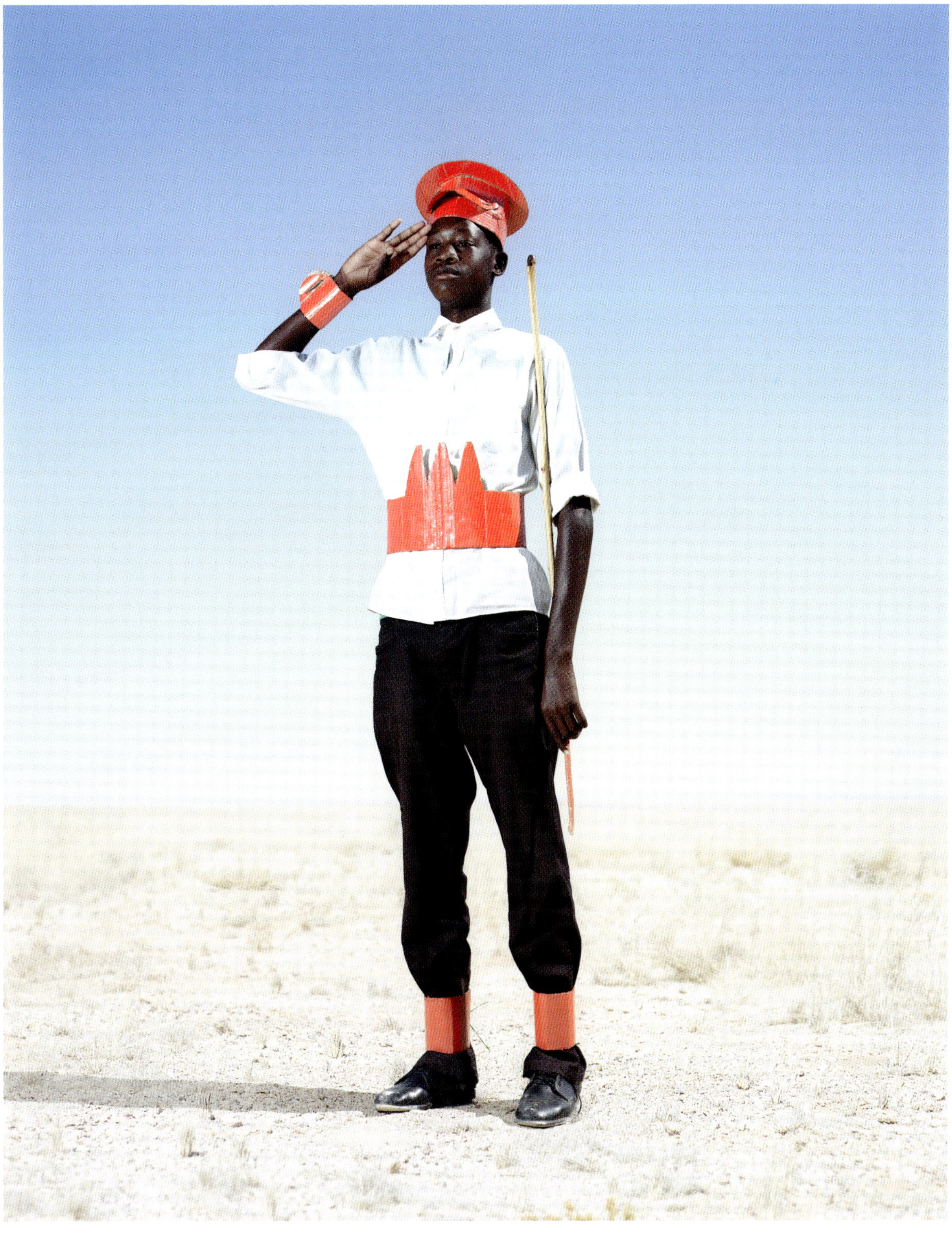

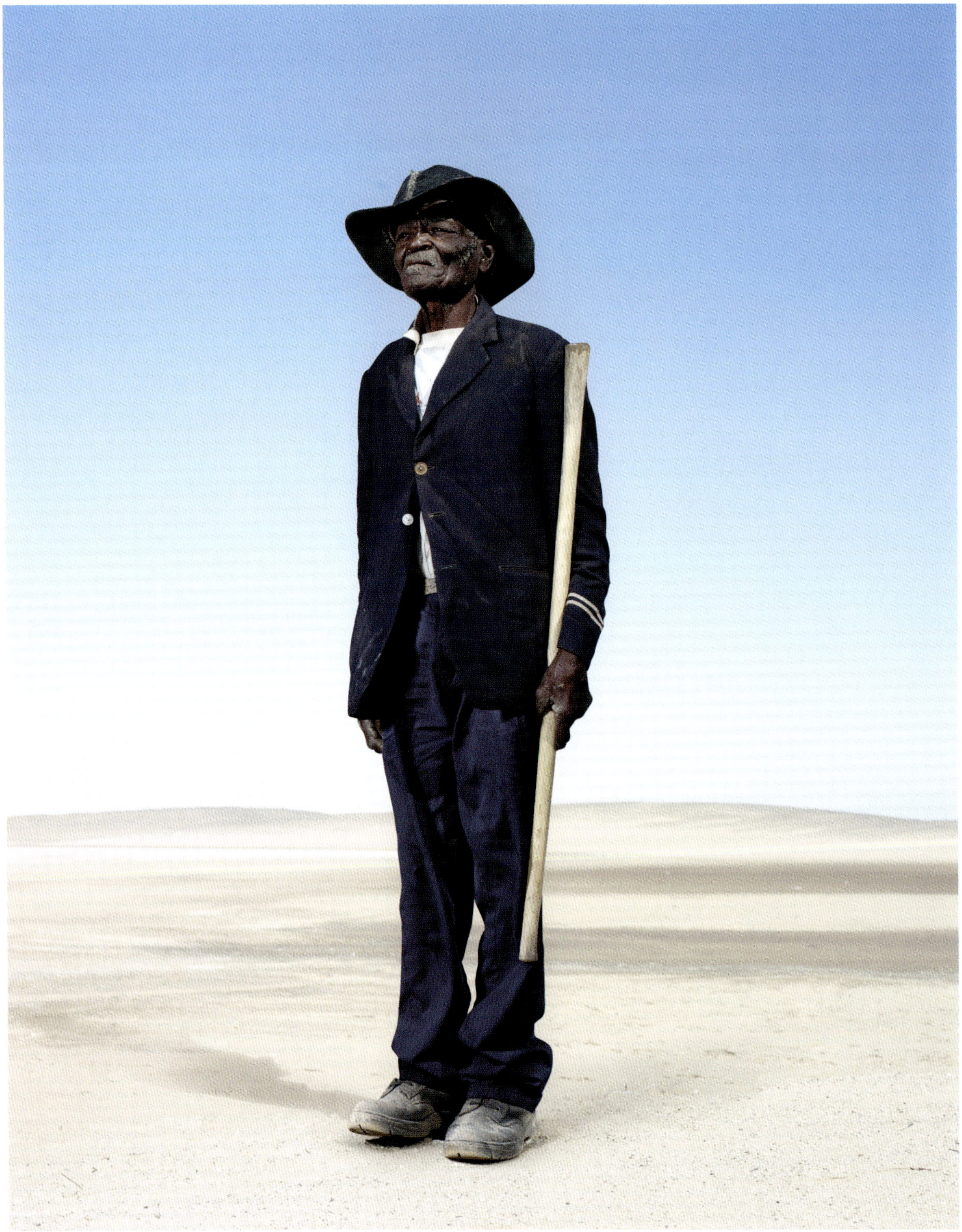

An *Otruppe* soldier in blue uniform. Many
Herero men carry a stick of some description.

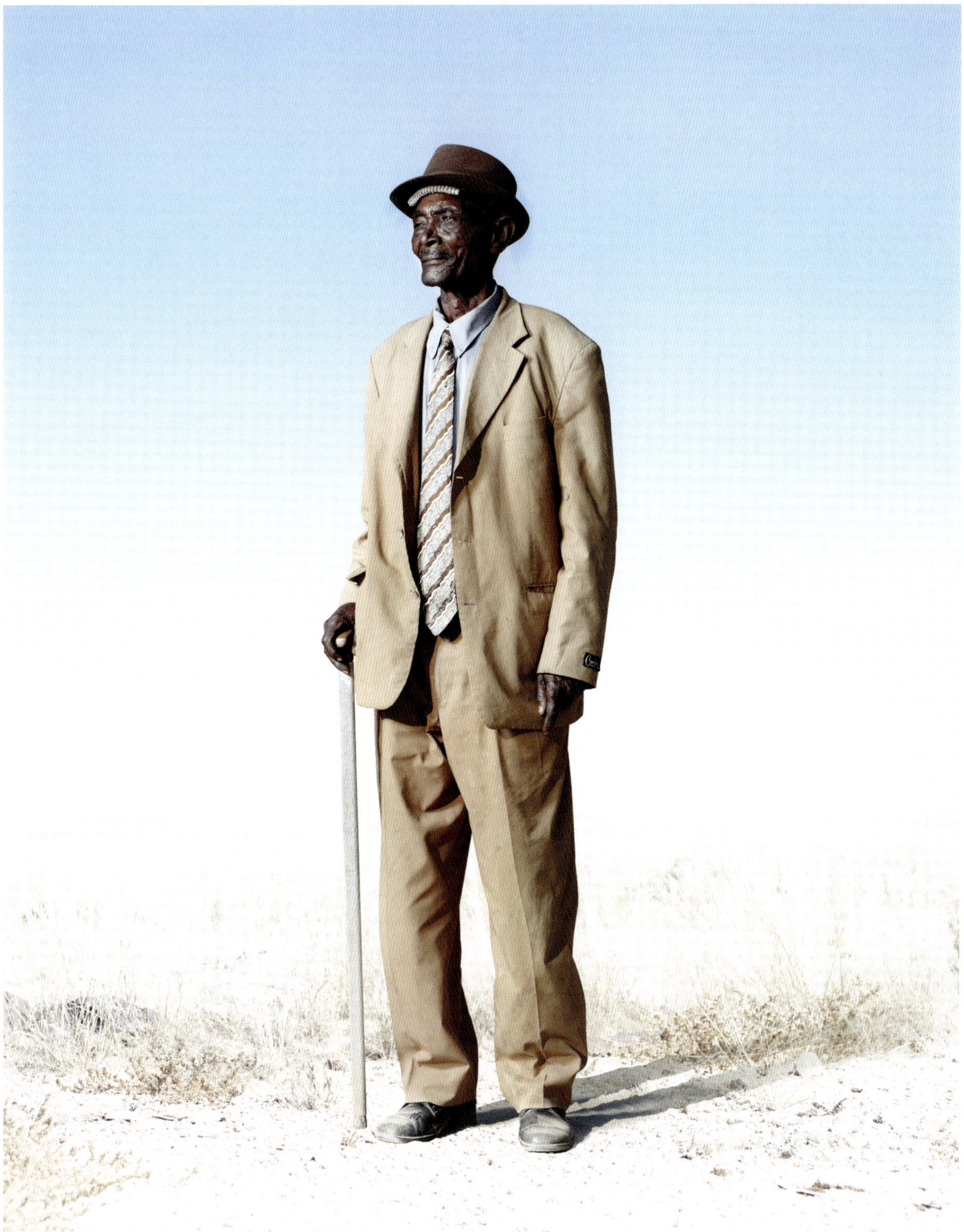

A Herero man in beige suit and chocolate-brown trilby.
The wearing of military uniforms is reserved
for ceremonial occasions and other special events.

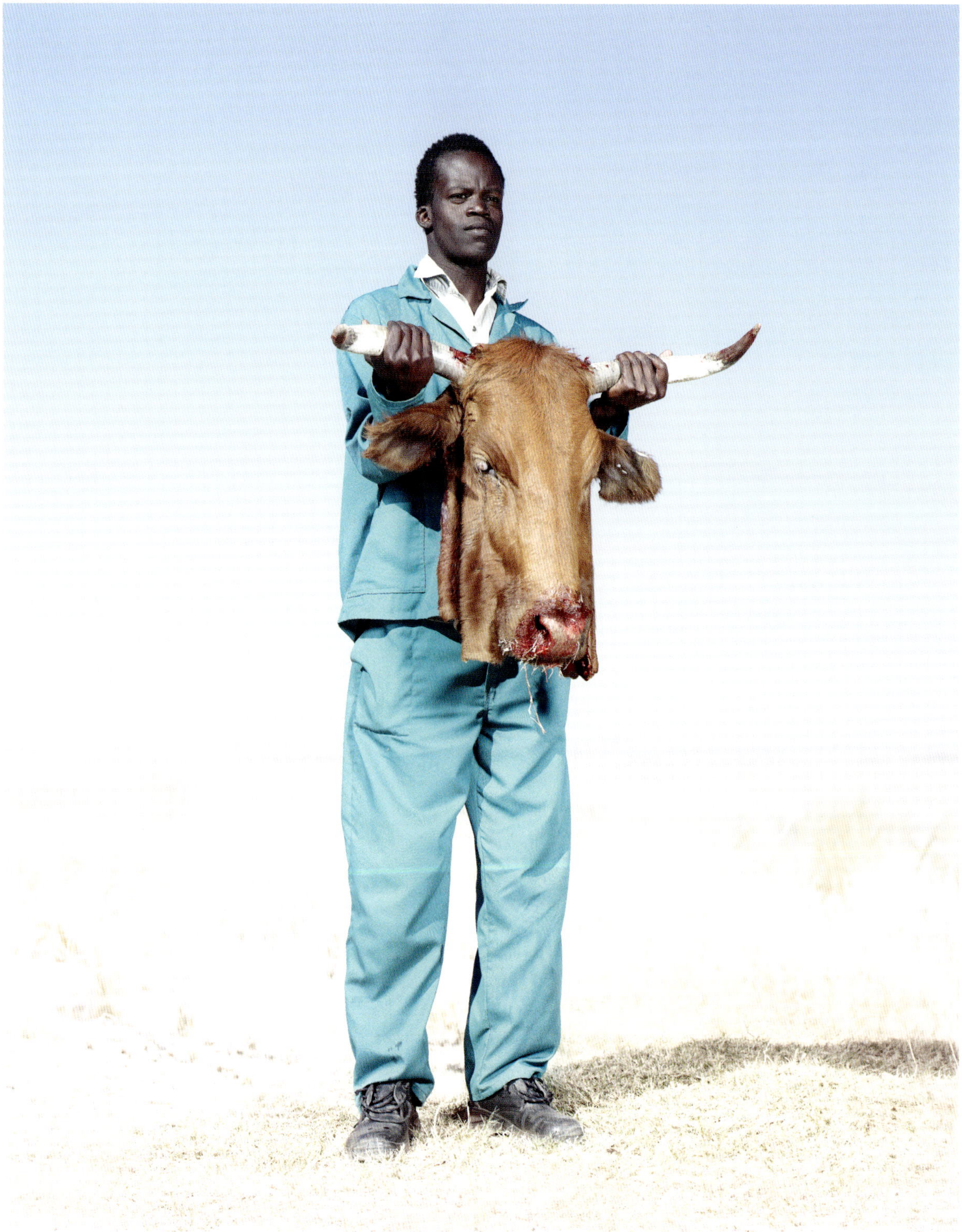

A Herero man holds the head of a freshly butchered cow, killed to supply meat for a funeral. The meat is boiled and given out to both funeral-goers and passers-by.

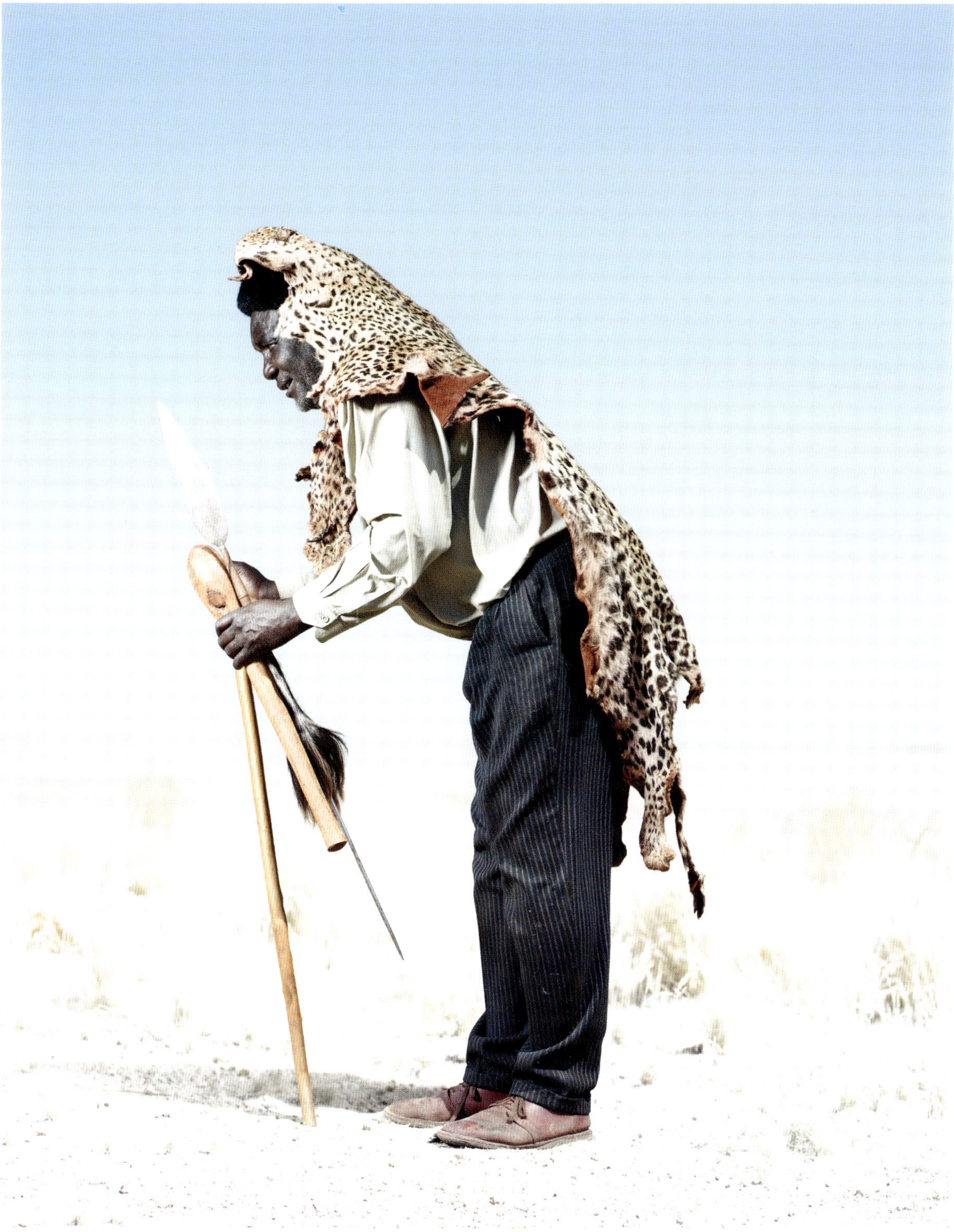

Draped in the skin of a leopard, a Herero man demonstrates a traditional battle stance. His weapons, also traditional, include a short spear and a hand club.

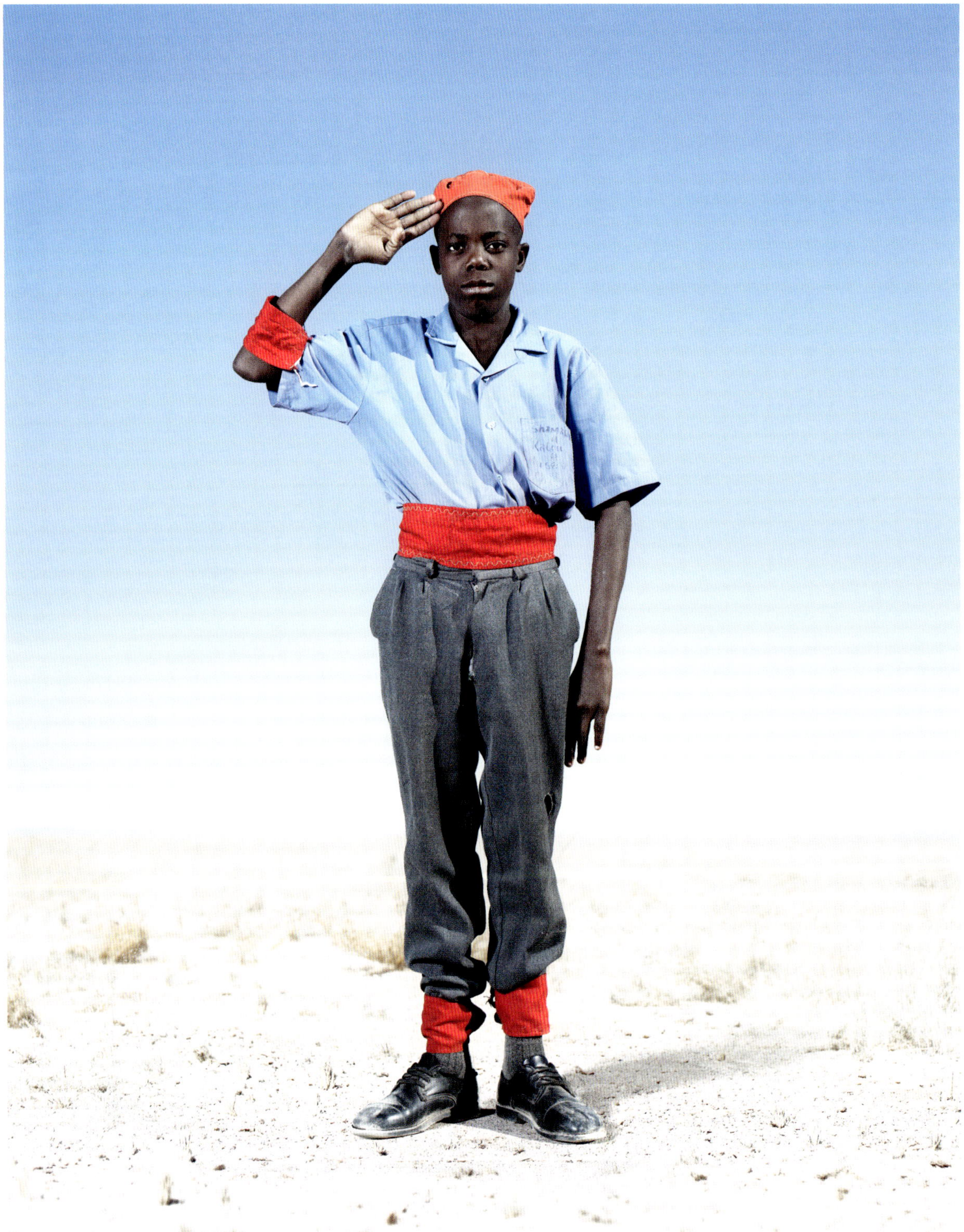

Two *Otjiserandu* cadets (above and opposite). As part of their training, the cadets must learn how to march. The orders are often given out in German, a reference to the *Schutztruppe*, the German colonial army.

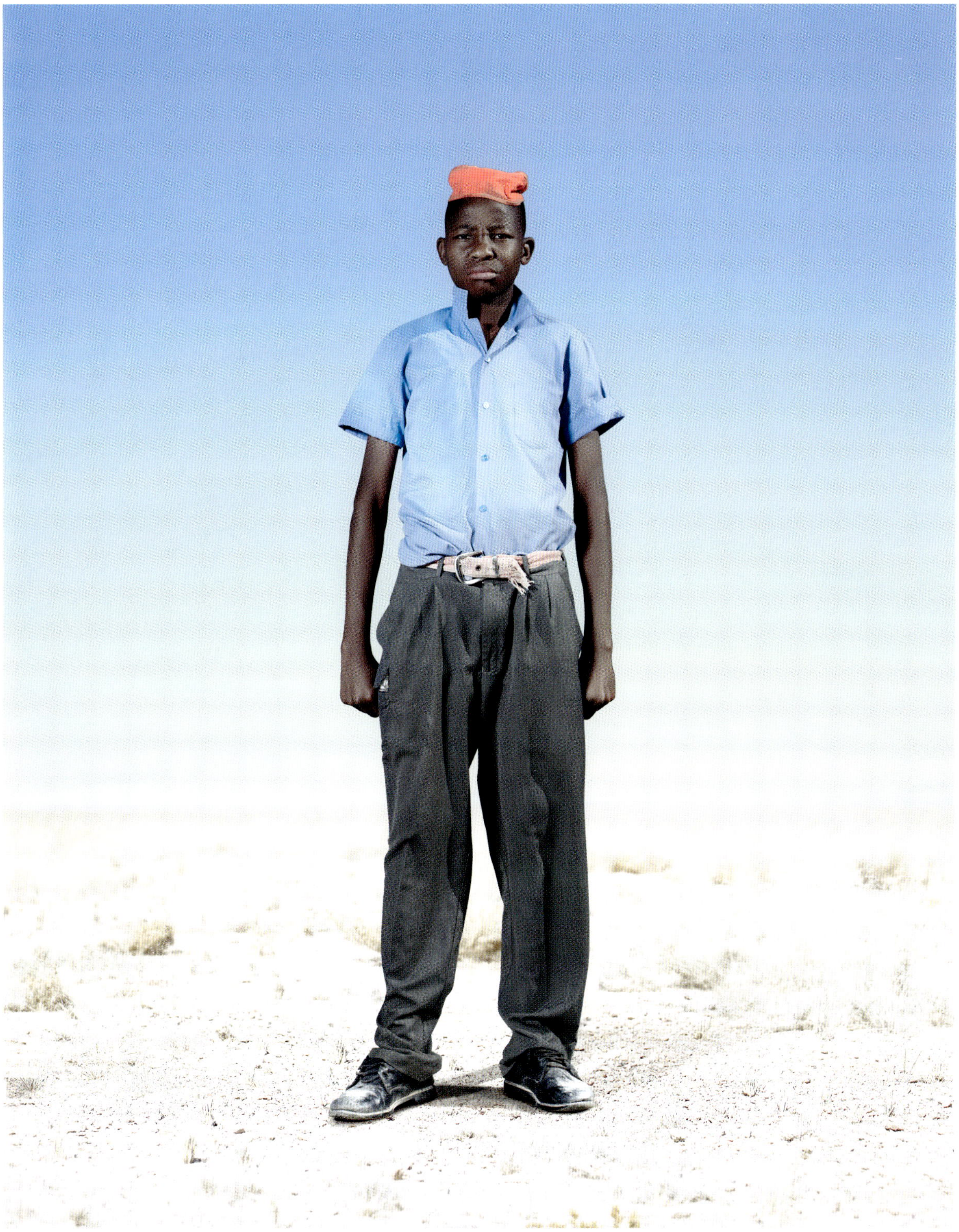

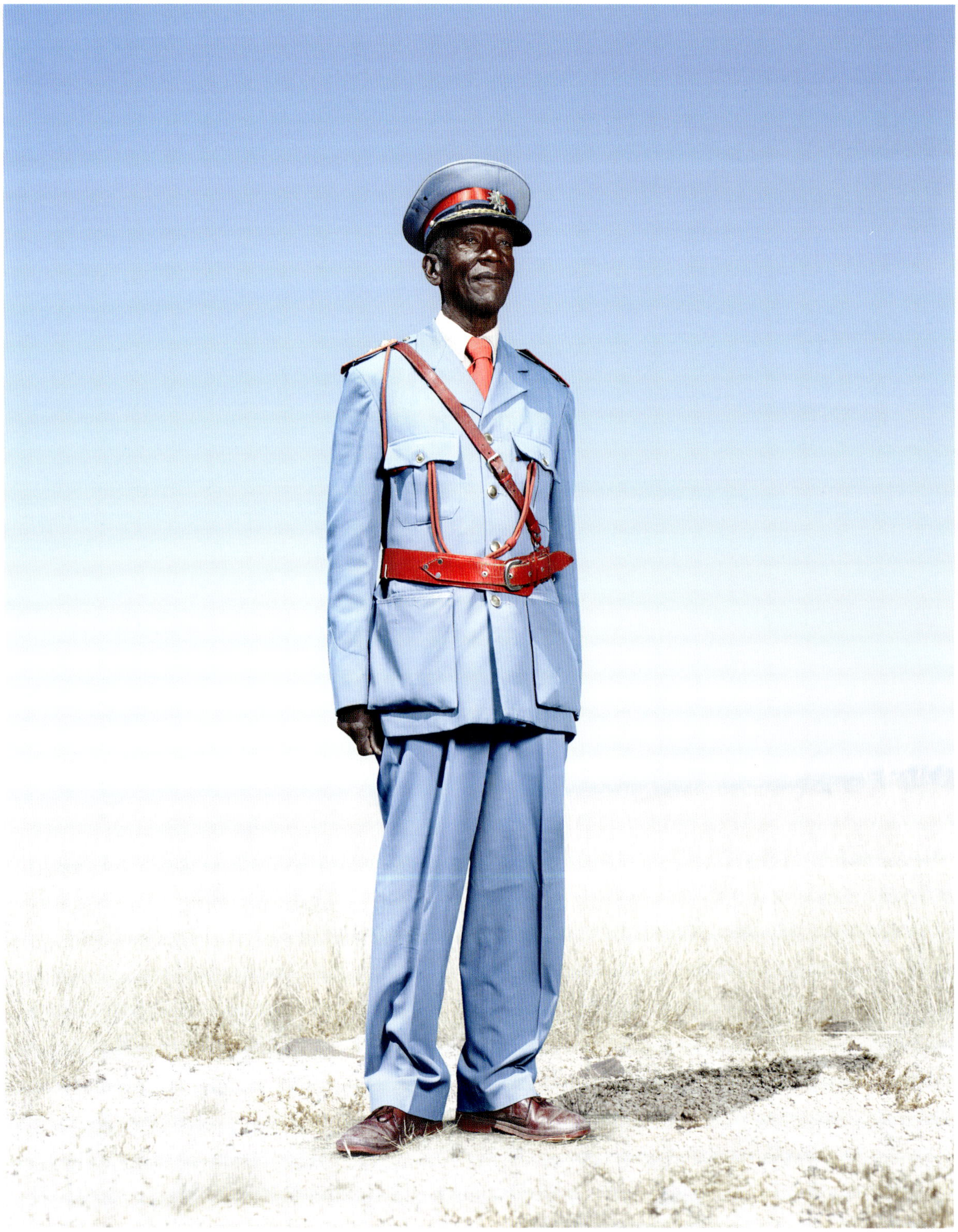

A senior *Otruppe* soldier (above) and a saluting cadet (opposite), both from the *Otjiserandu* section.

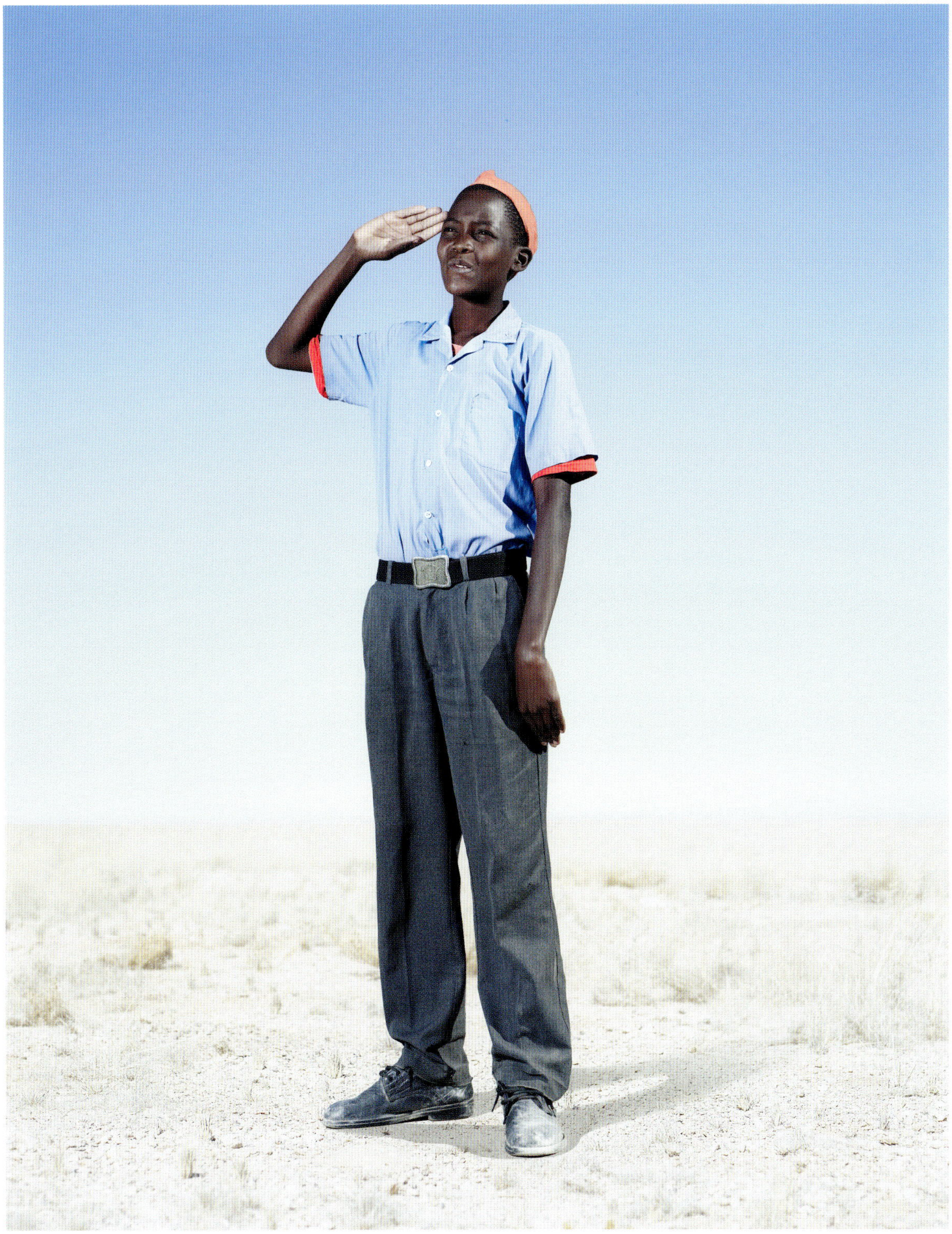

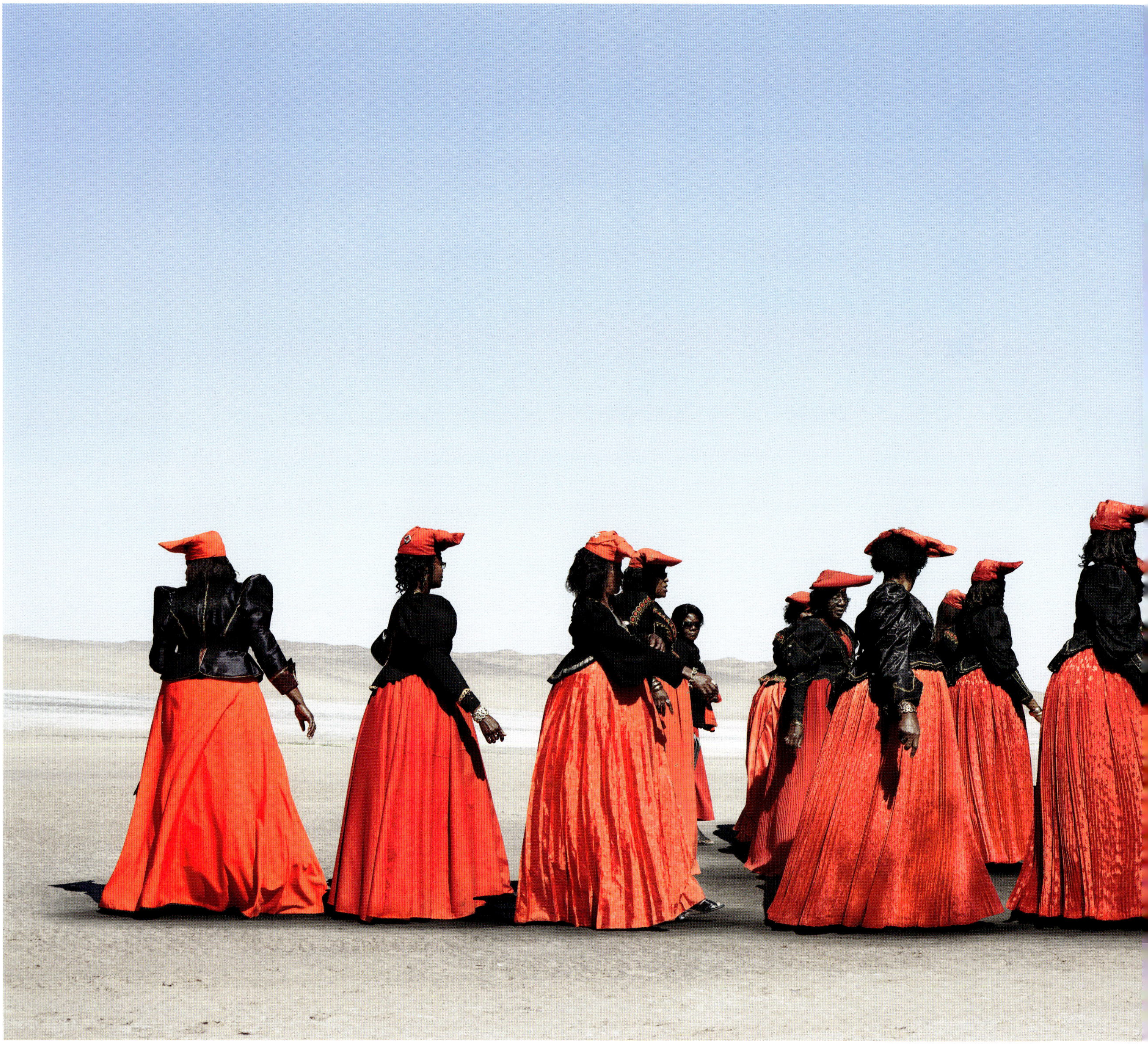

Conspicuous by their presence, two women from the *Otjigrine* section of the *Otruppe* march alongside a group of women from the *Otjiserandu*. The women's formal, or 'military', dresses are worn at such ceremonies and festivals as Herero Day, held every August in Okahandja to commemorate Herero chiefs of the past.

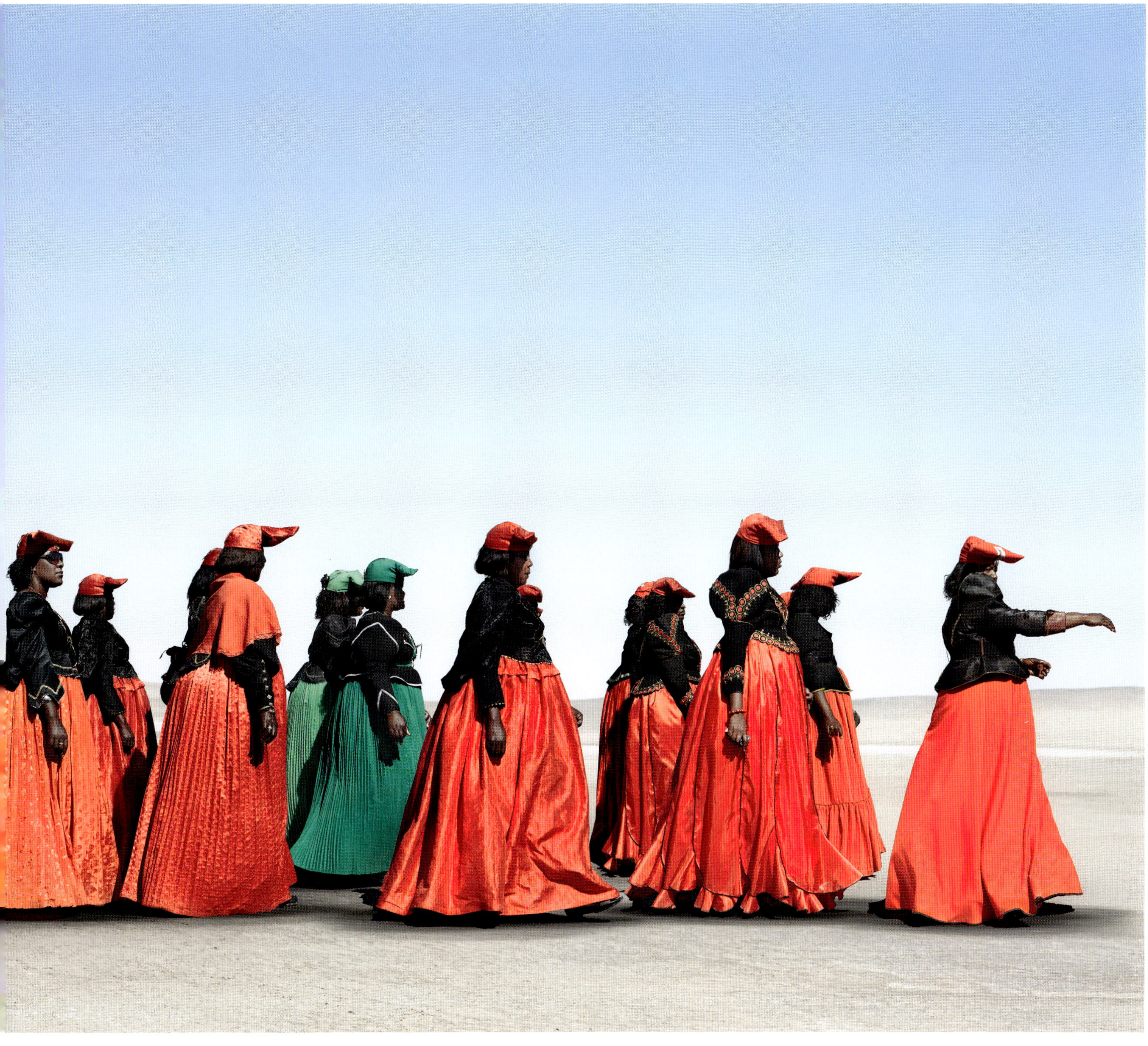

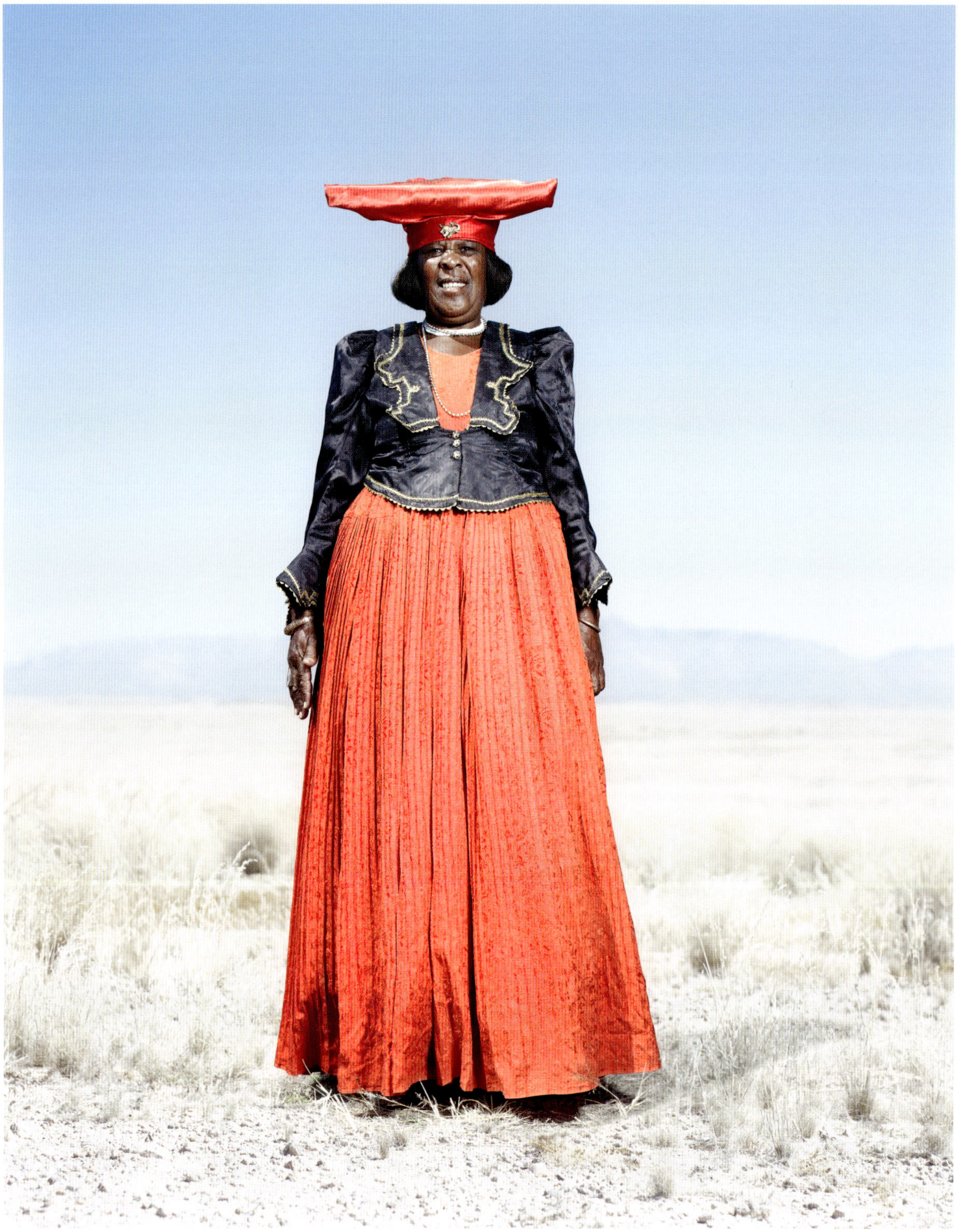

A Herero woman of the *Otjiserandu* in her formal dress.

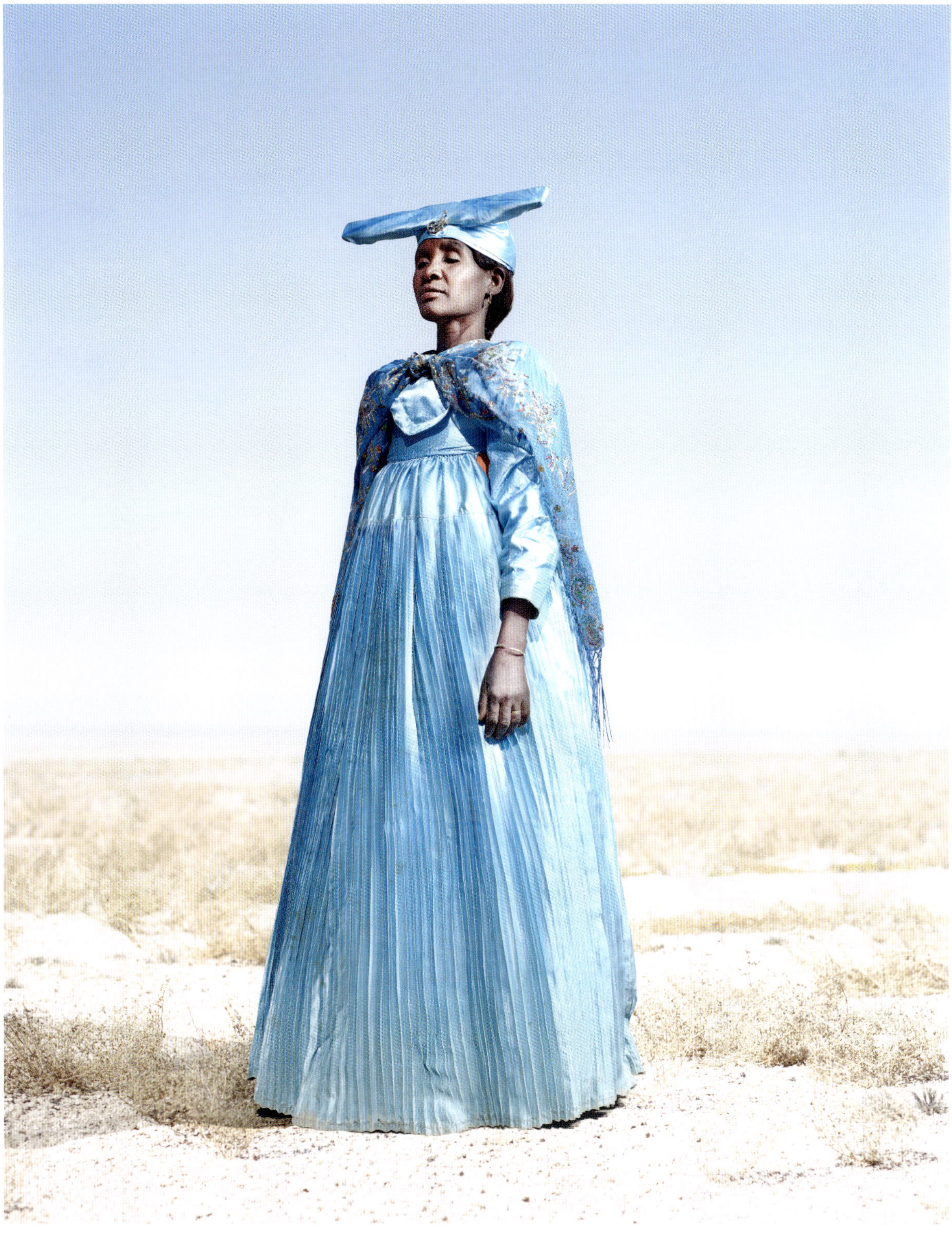

The striking blue material of this woman's dress would probably have been purchased in one of the larger Namibian towns. The dresses themselves, however, are often made by the wearer.

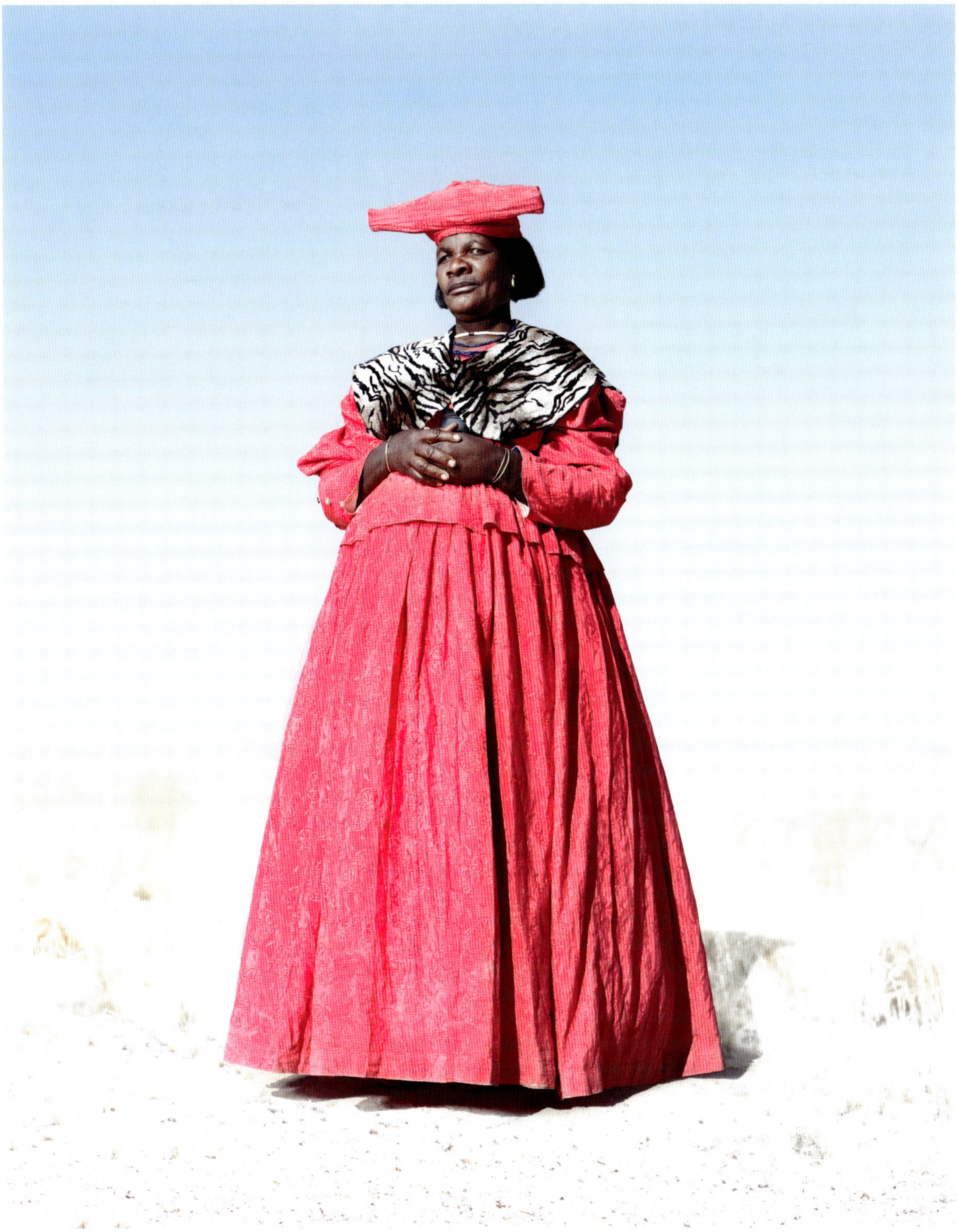

The rounded shape of the formal Herero long dress, here accompanied by a zebra-skin shawl, symbolizes the feminine, life-giving aspects of the cow. It also induces in the wearer a regular and stately gait, another reference to the cattle that are so important to Herero society.

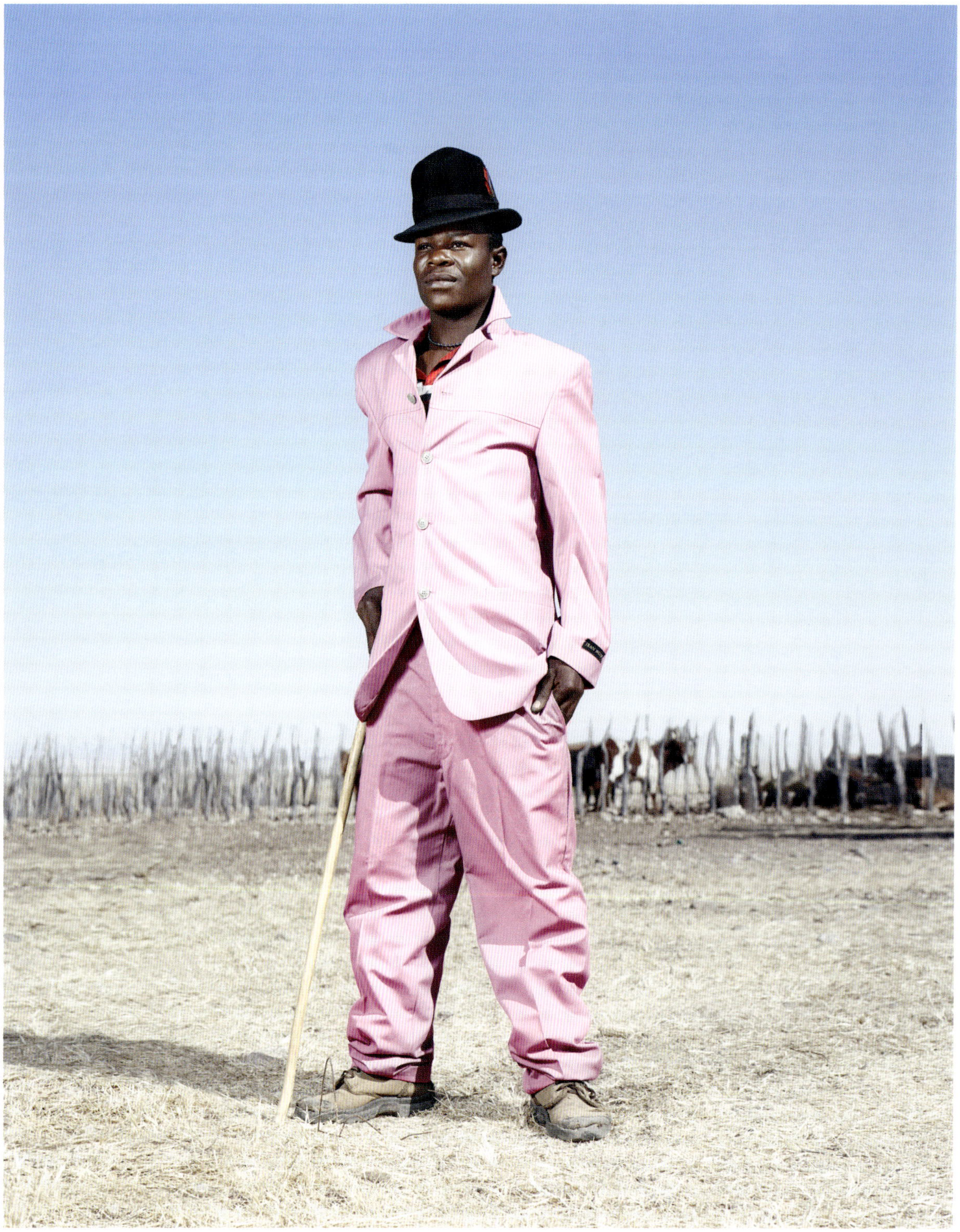

A young Herero man, resplendent in pink suit and bowler-style hat, in front of a cattle *kraal*.

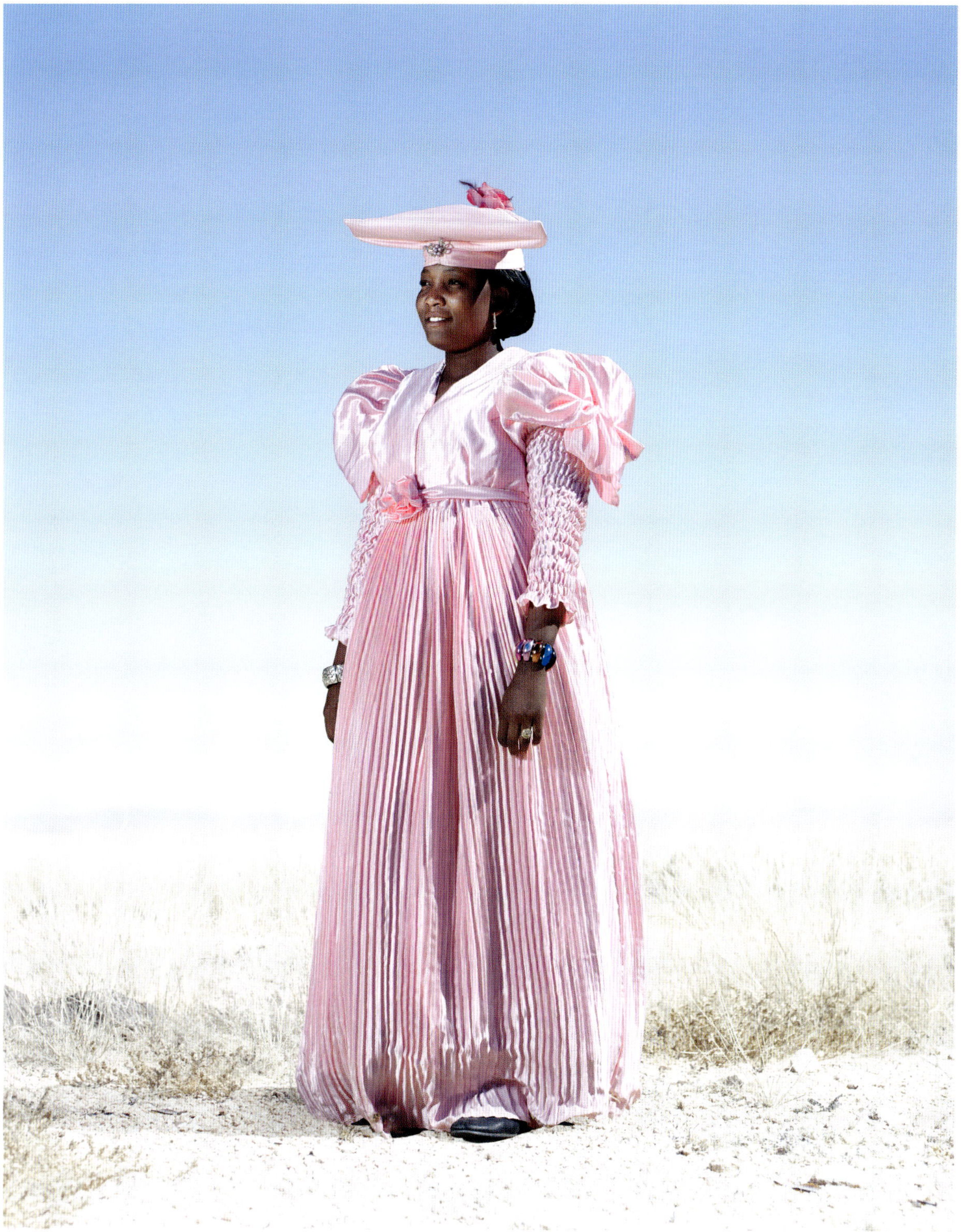

This woman is dressed to attend a funeral. Herero funerals can last for several days, with funeral-goers, who often travel long distances in order to pay their respects, camping at the funeral site.

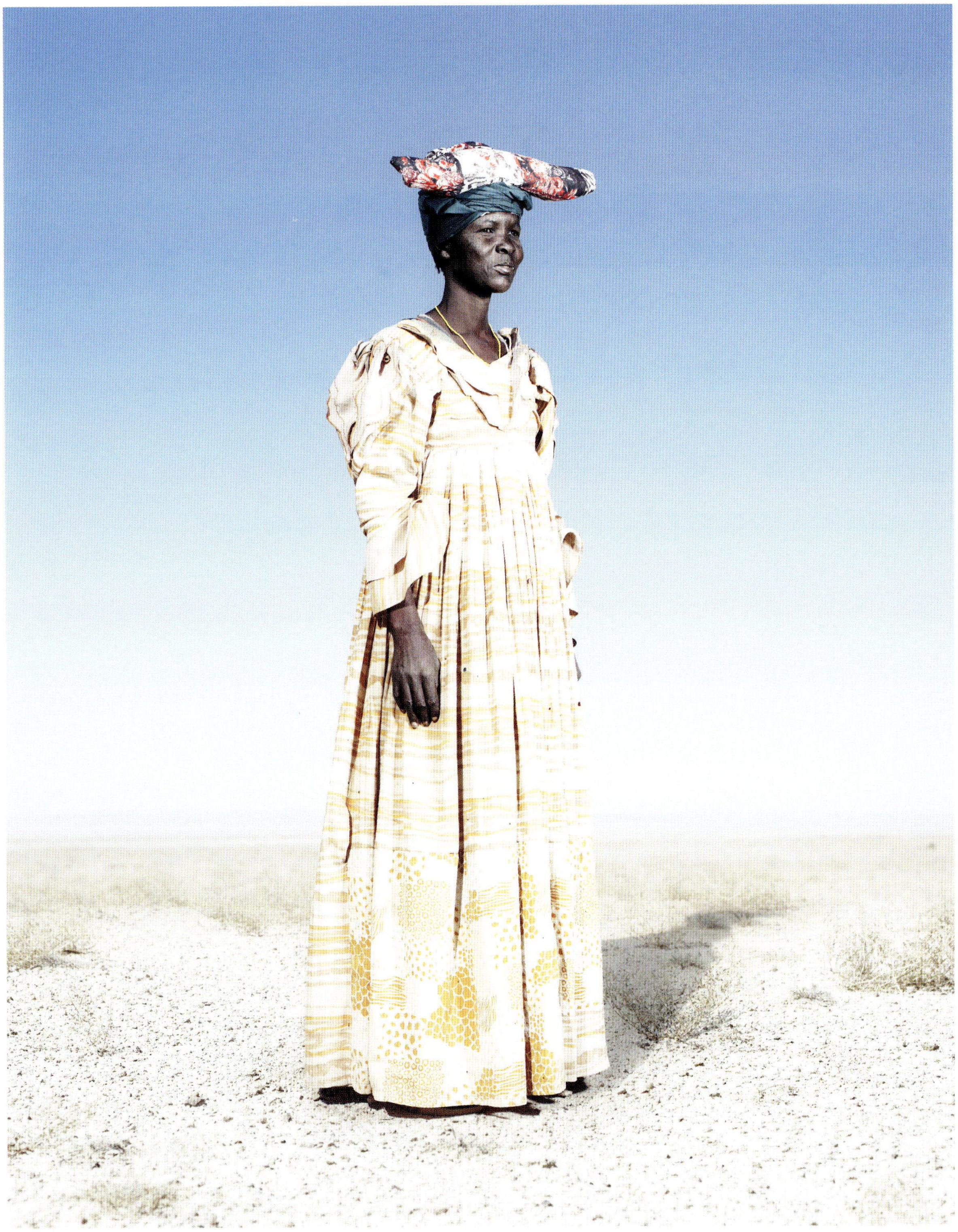

A Herero woman in a patterned long dress. The distinctive Herero dress is worn every day of the year, no matter what the weather. In the summer, temperatures can reach 50°C (122°F).

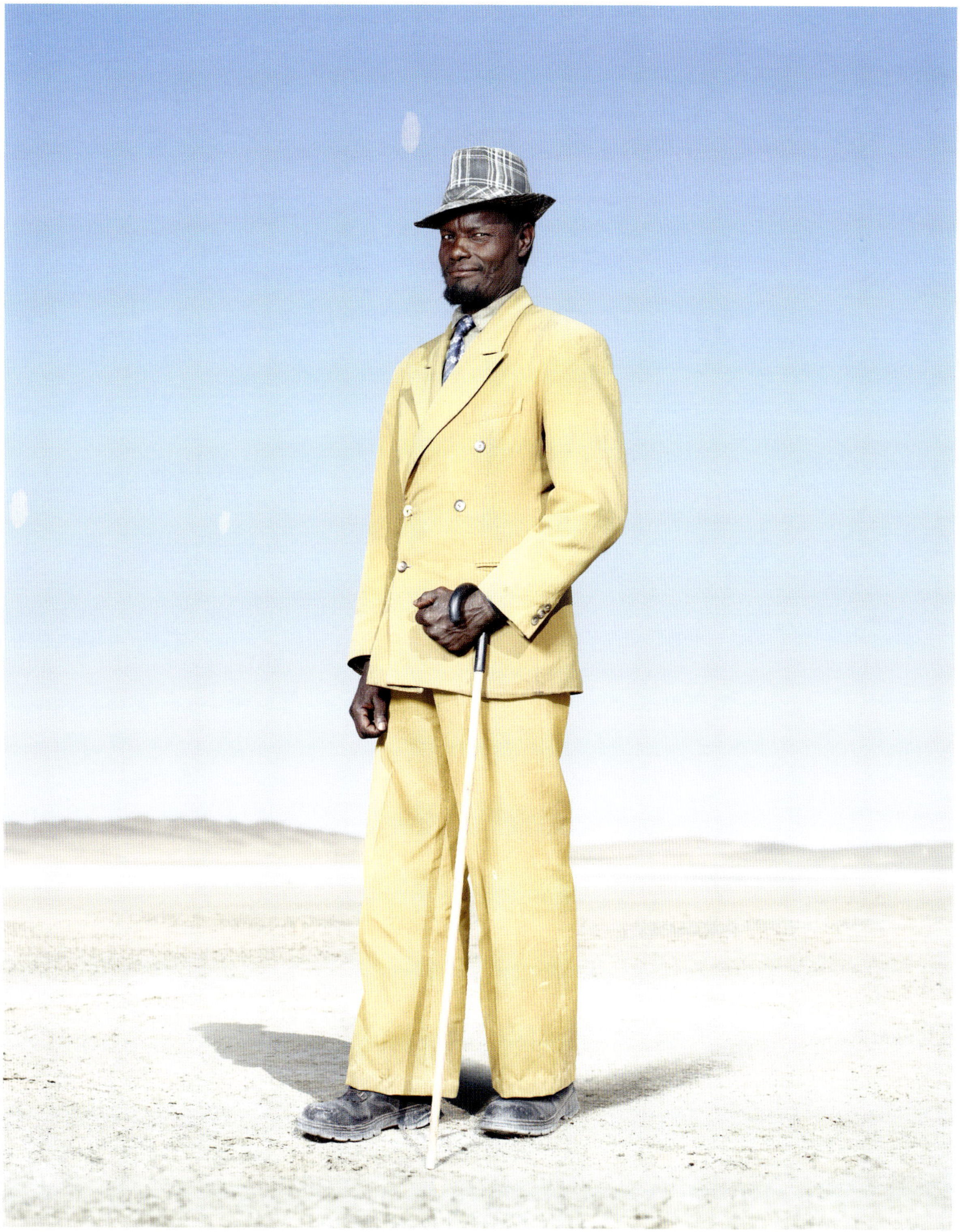

The tradition of wearing formal attire is maintained by most Herero elders, such as this man in yellow double-breasted suit and check trilby. It is, however, noticeably in decline among younger Herero men, who tend to favour jeans and a T-shirt.

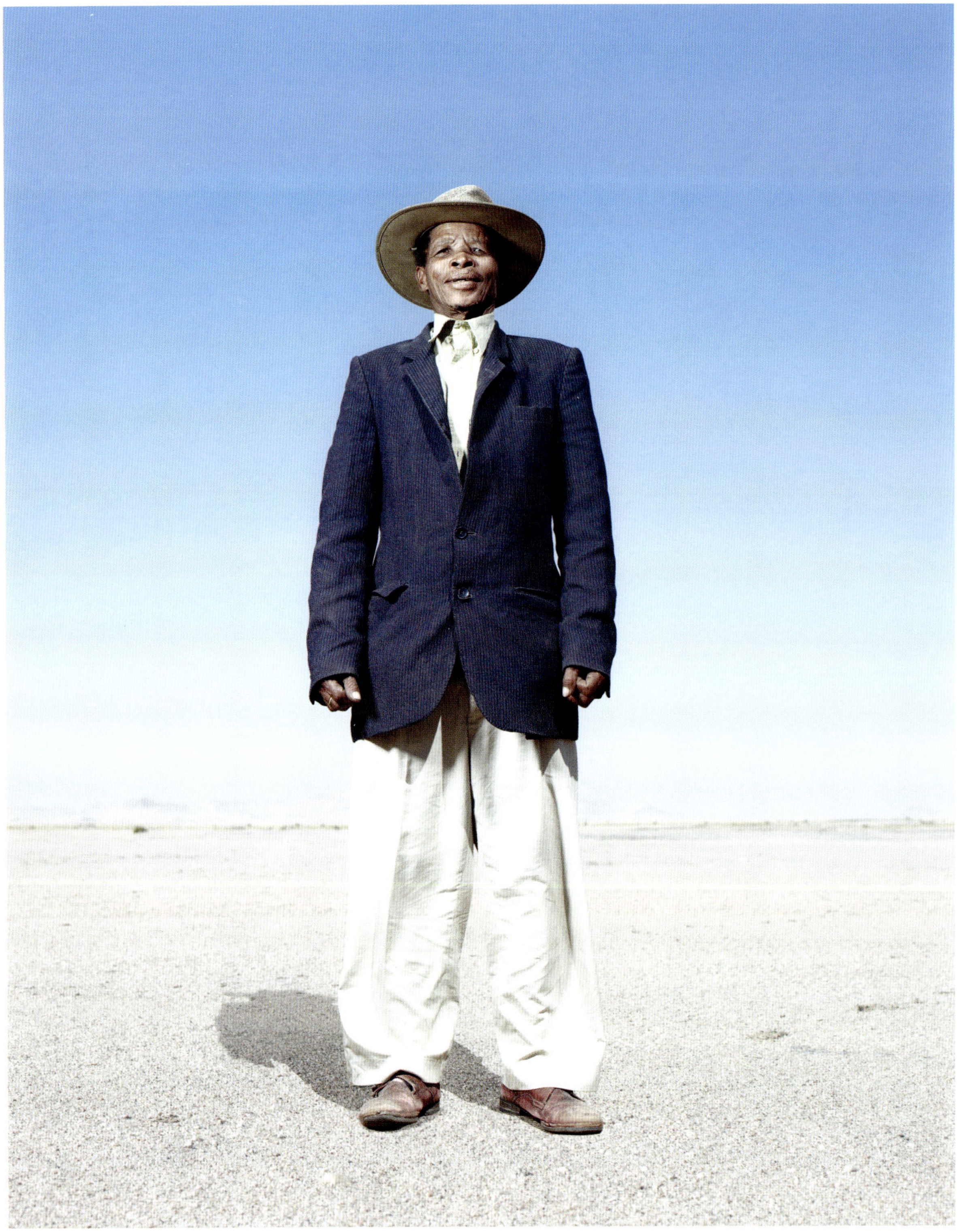

A San leader from the Omaheke region of Namibia, dressed in a suit inspired by the Herero. The San are the oldest recorded inhabitants of southern Africa.

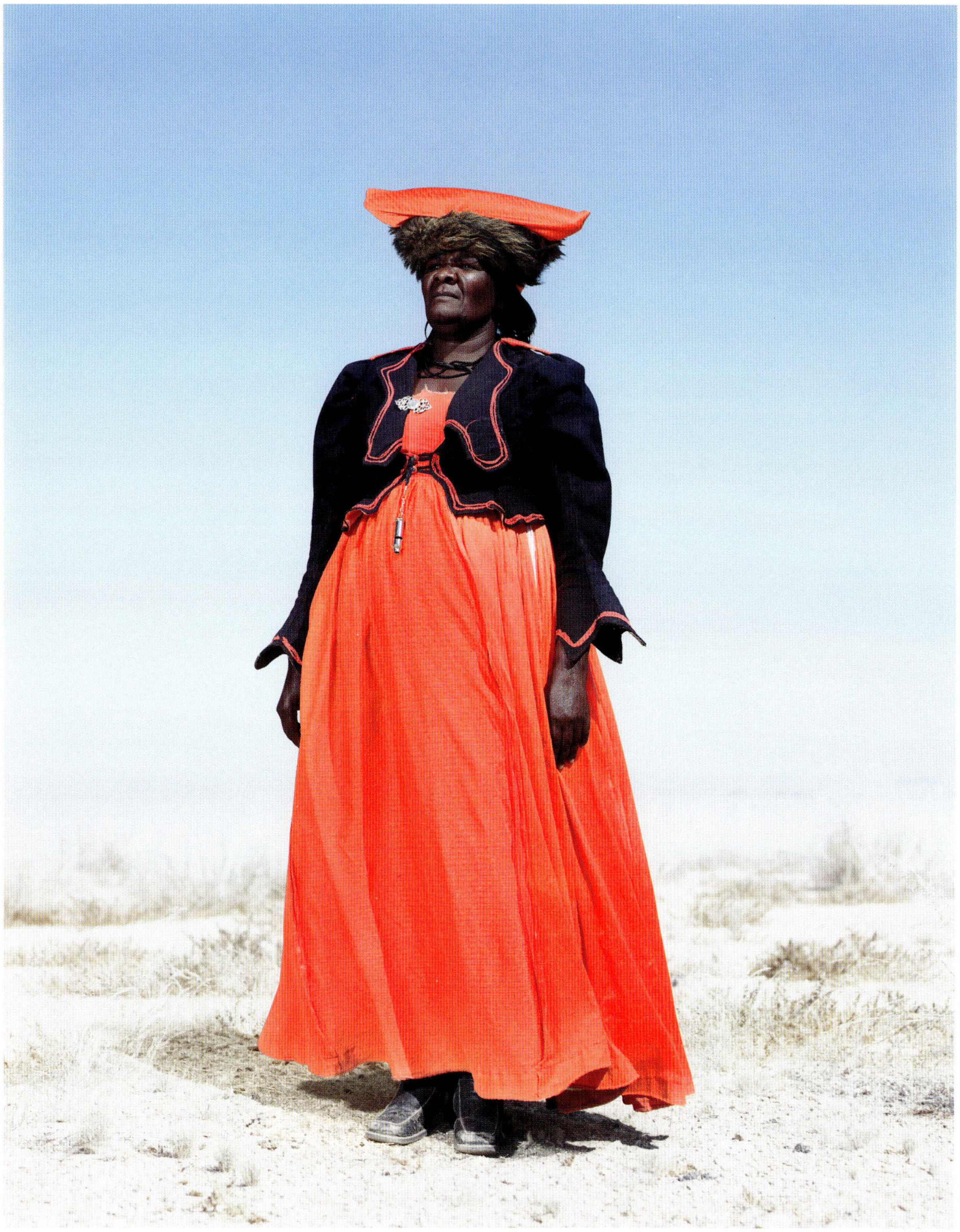

A Herero woman from the *Otjiserandu* section
of the *Otruppe* in her formal dress.

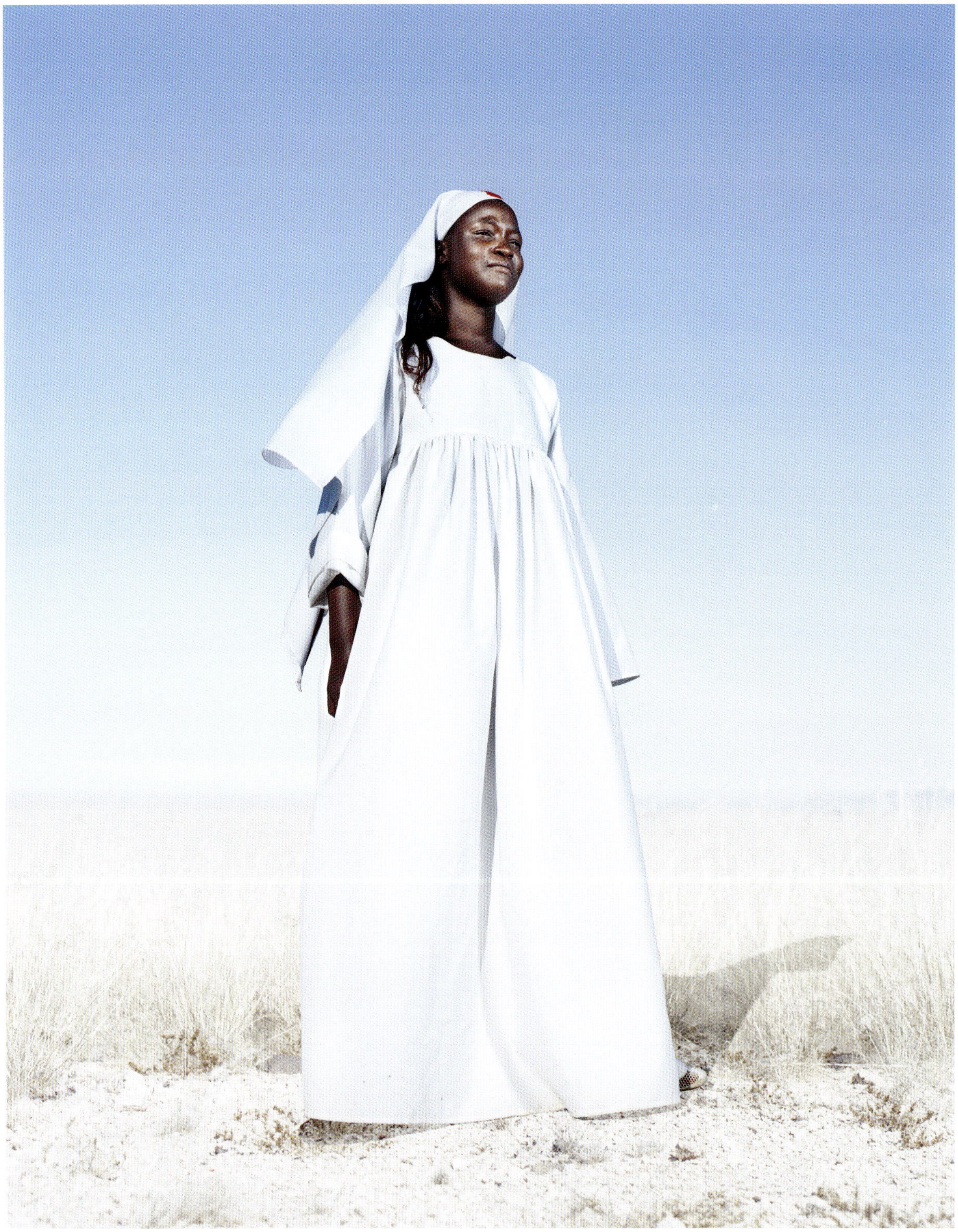

A Herero nun from the Kunene region of Namibia. Although Christianity is the country's official religion, it is often combined with or practised alongside more traditional ancestor-worship.

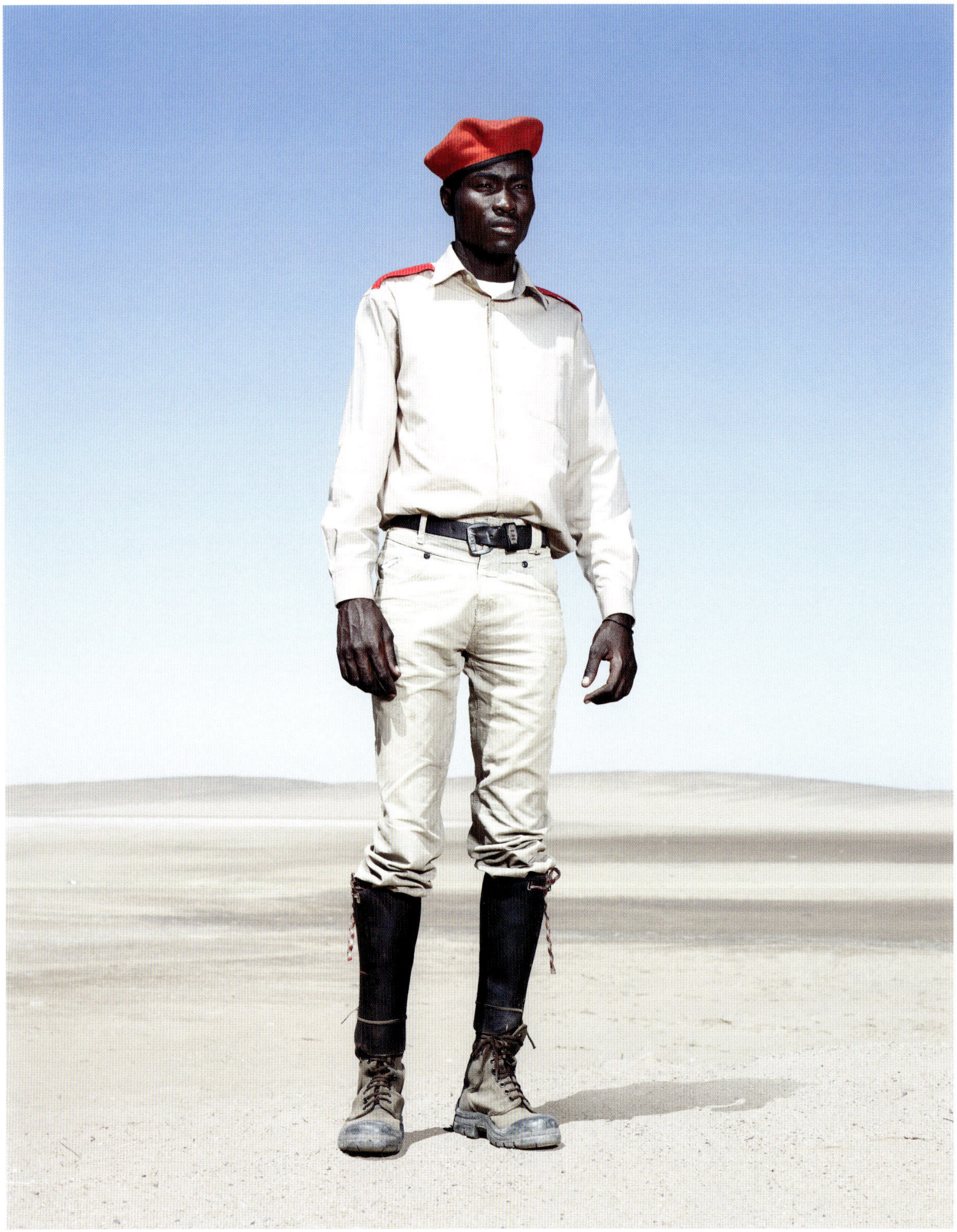

The red features of the uniform worn by this *Otruppe* cavalryman signal his membership of the *Otjiserandu* section.

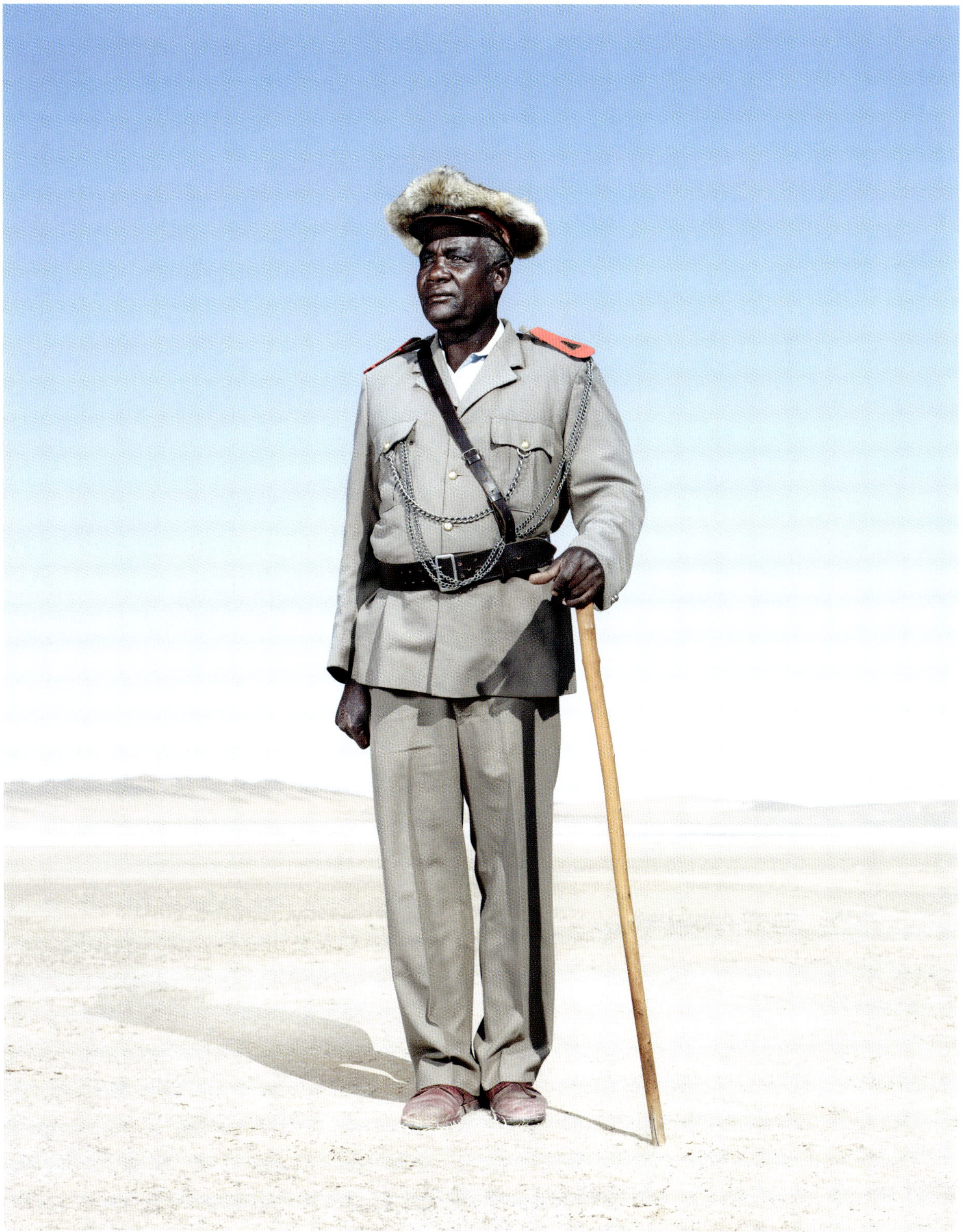

A senior *Otruppe* soldier. With the establishment of the *Otruppe* movement shortly after the end of the First World War, military uniforms became particularly important to the Herero. Some members wore uniforms left behind by, or captured from, the *Schutztruppe*, the German colonial army.

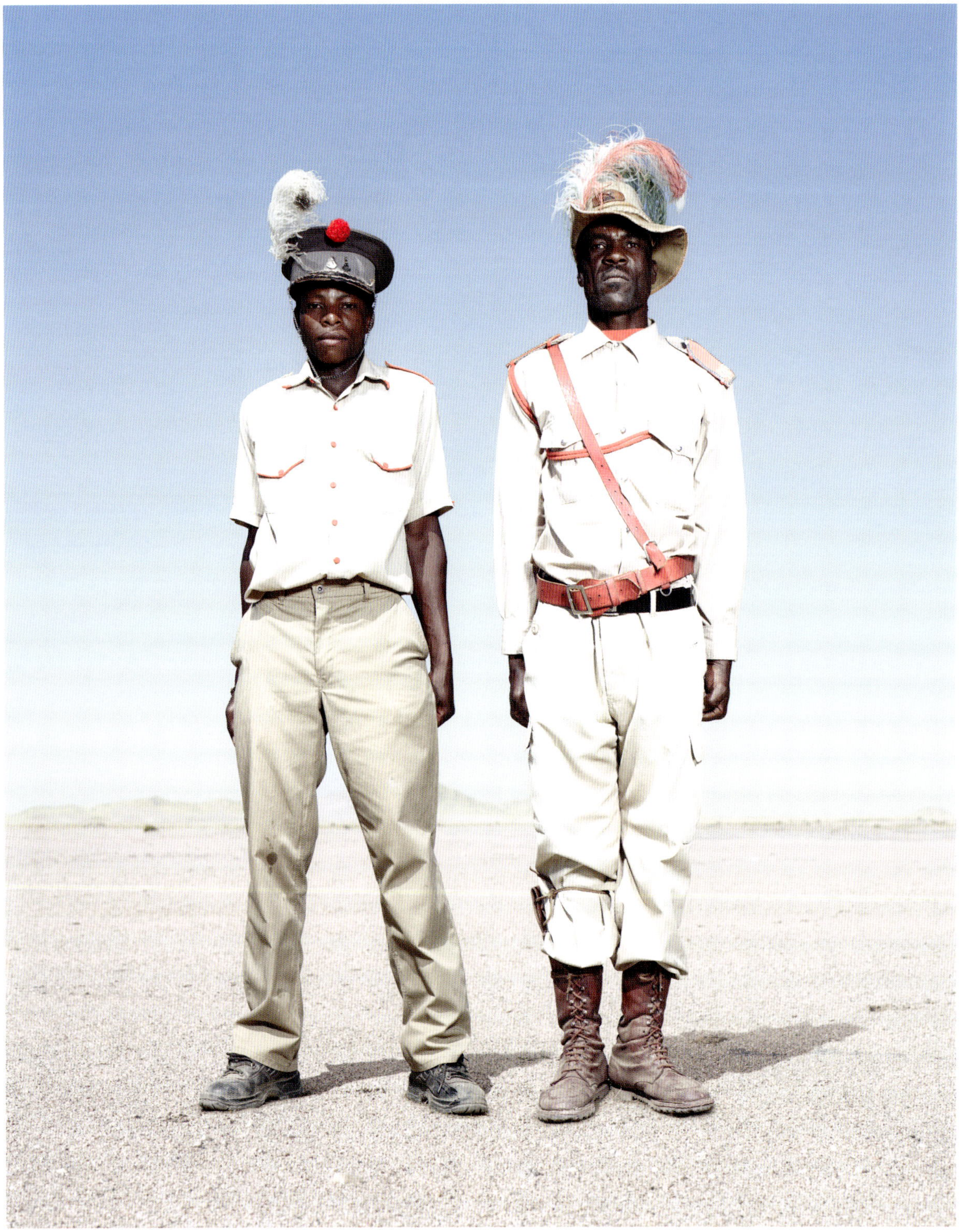

Two *Otruppe* cavalrymen. Their hats are adorned with coloured ostrich feathers.

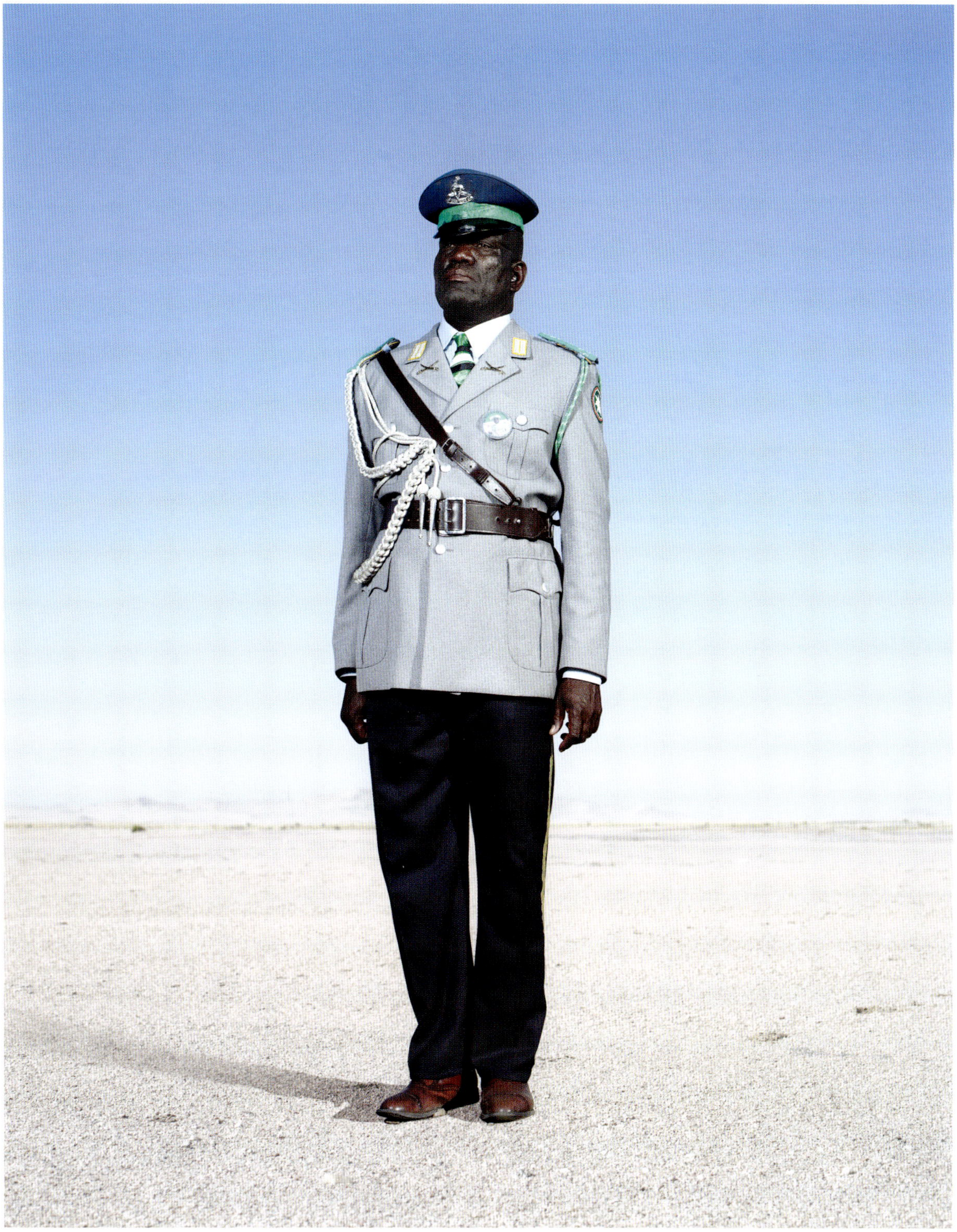

A soldier from the *Otjigrine* section of the *Otruppe*.

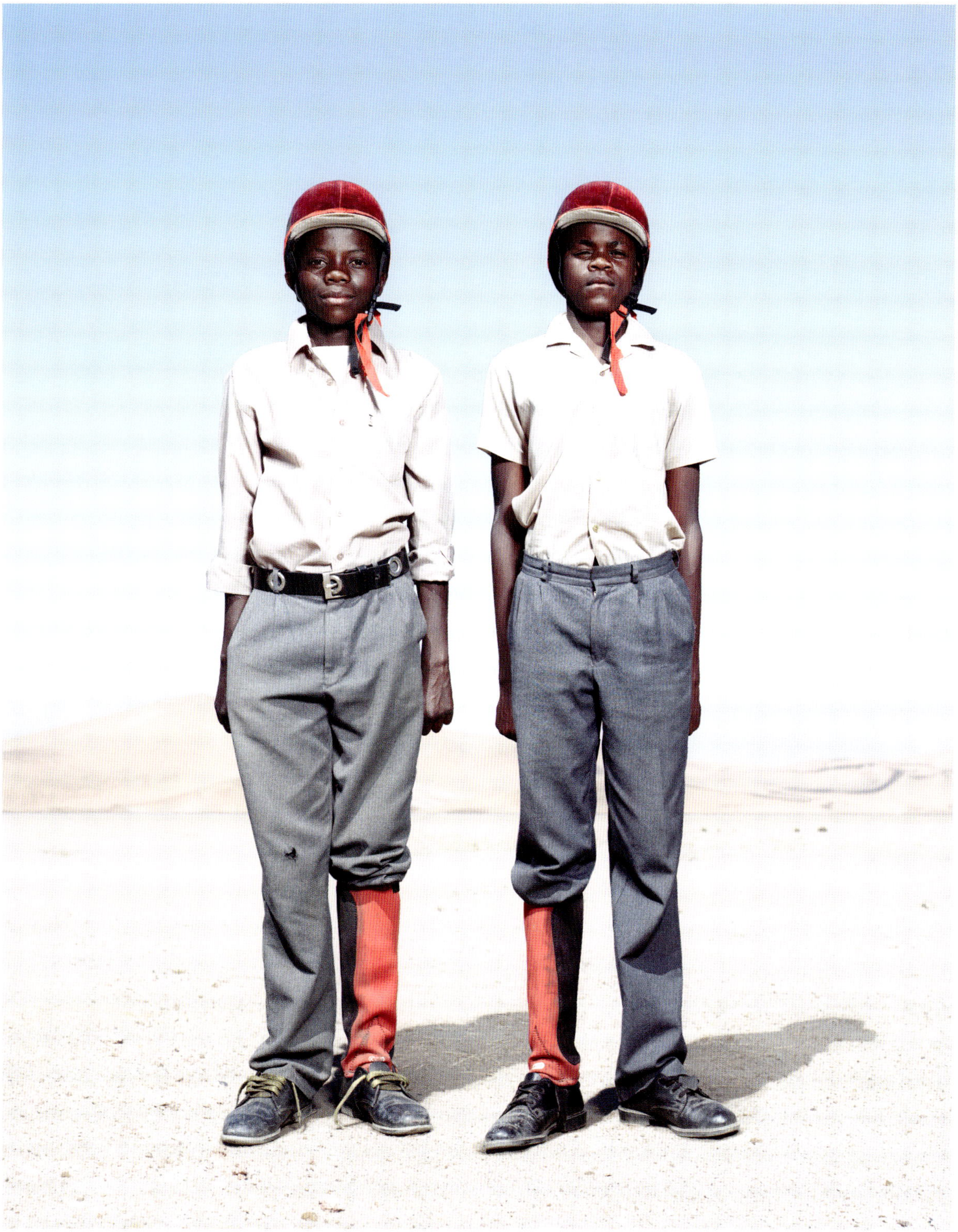

Two *Otruppe* cavalry cadets in helmets – and
a shared pair of gaiters.

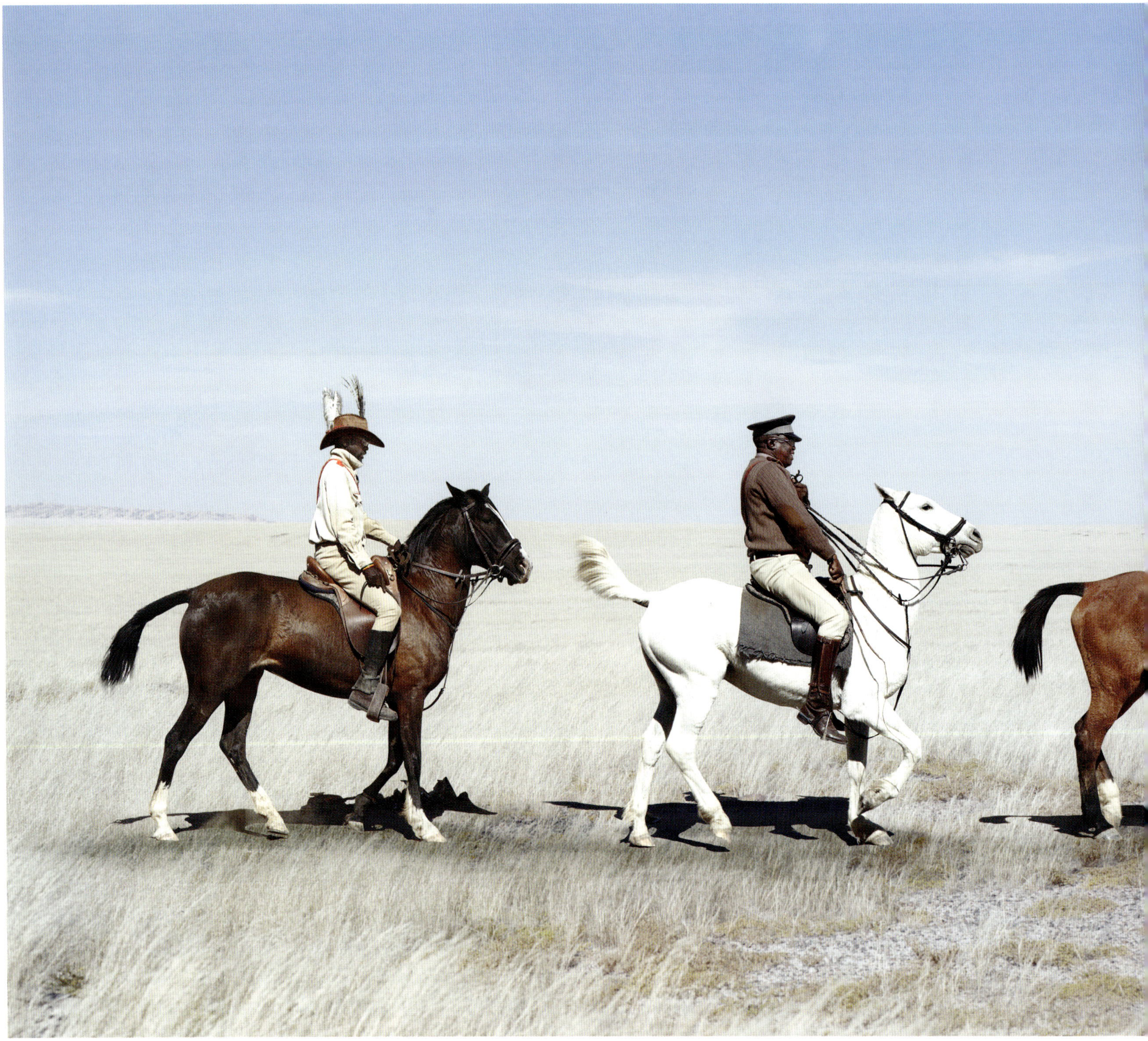

A group of *Otruppe* cavalrymen on horseback. Equestrian displays can be seen at such festivals and ceremonies as Herero Day (see page 62).

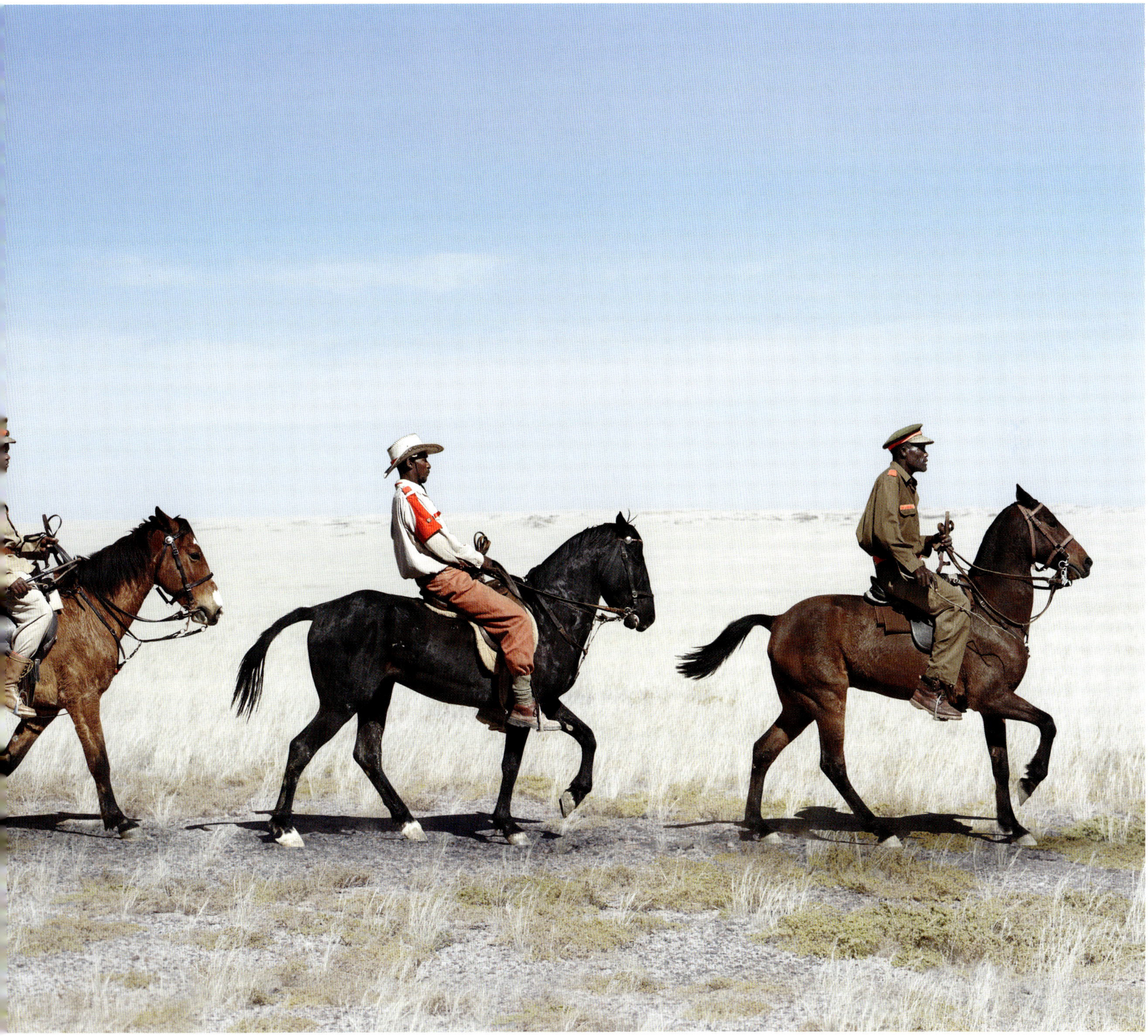

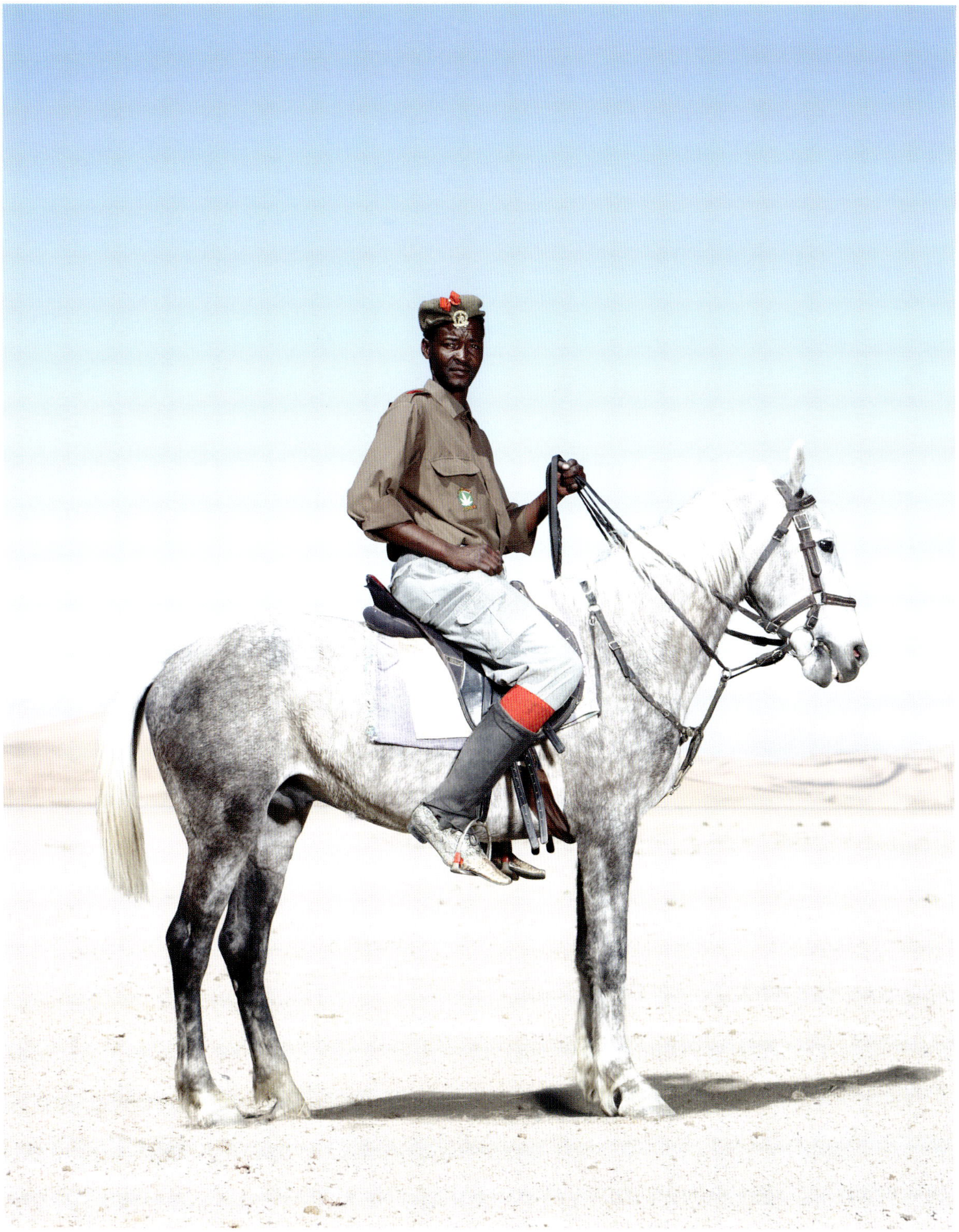

An *Otruppe* cavalryman on horseback. Since the introduction of horses into Namibia in the 1850s by migrants and traders from the Cape, the Herero have become skilled horsemen.

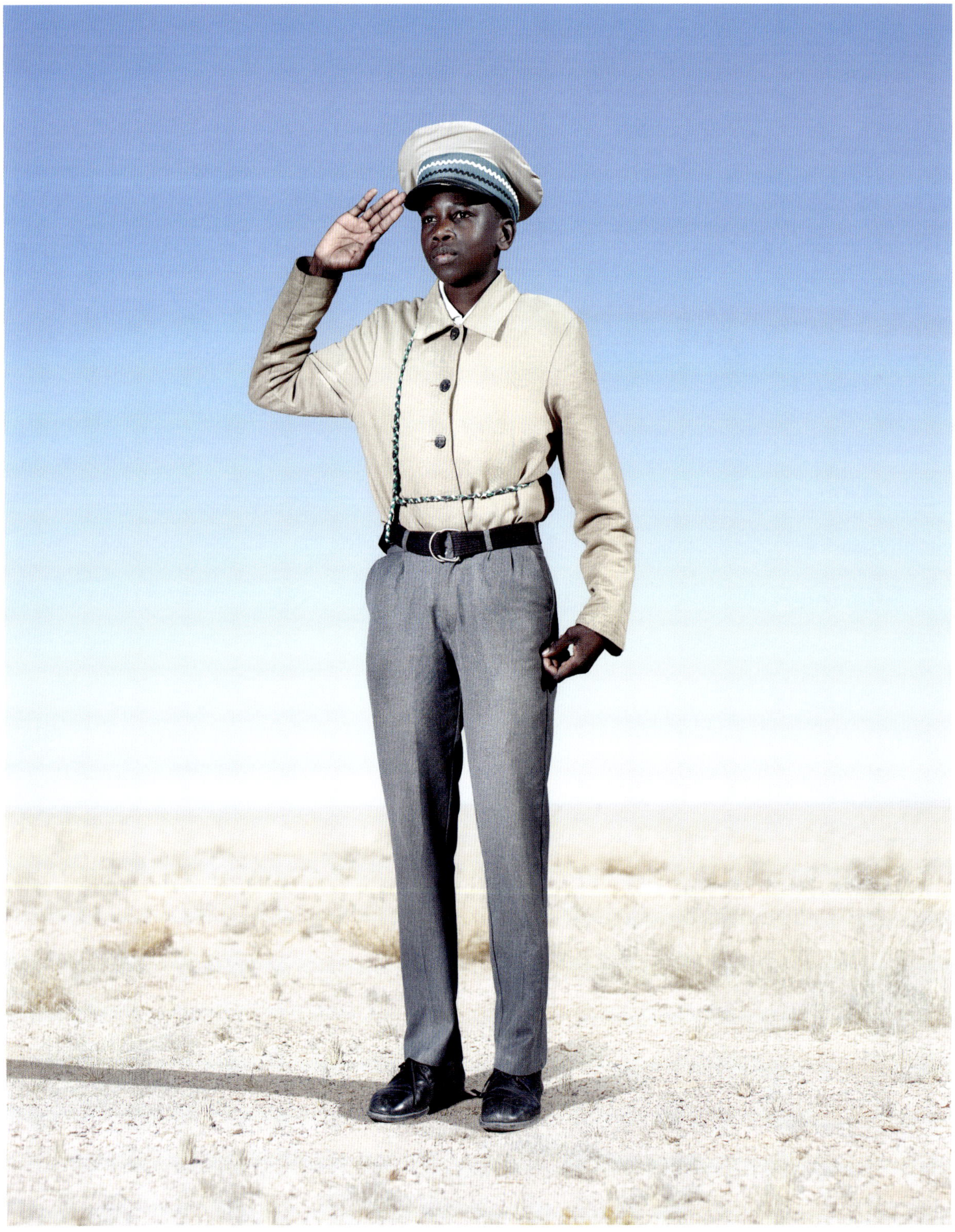

A cadet from the *Otjigrine* section of the *Otruppe*.

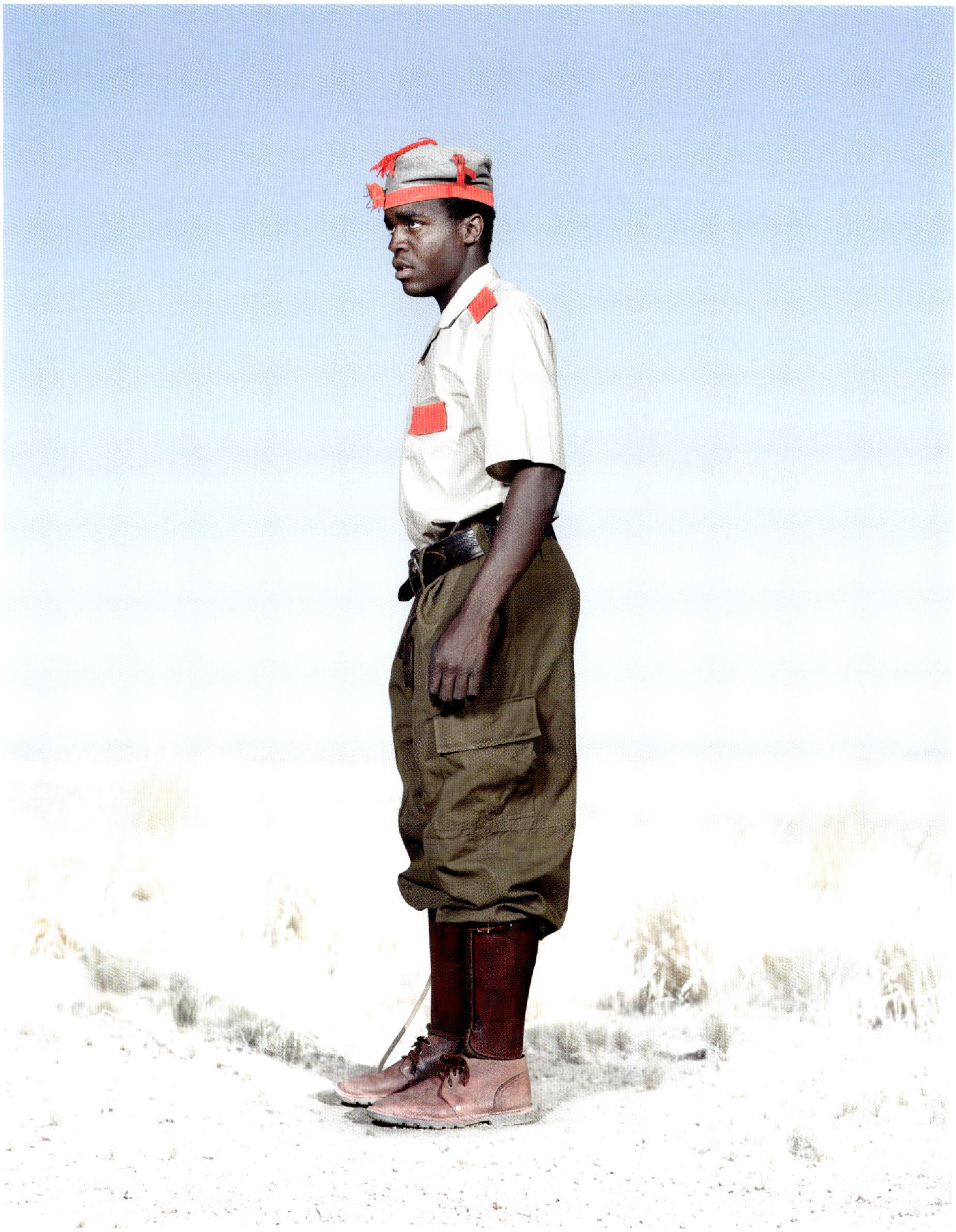

An *Otruppe* cavalryman of the *Otjiserandu* section.
Part of his whip can be seen by his right foot.

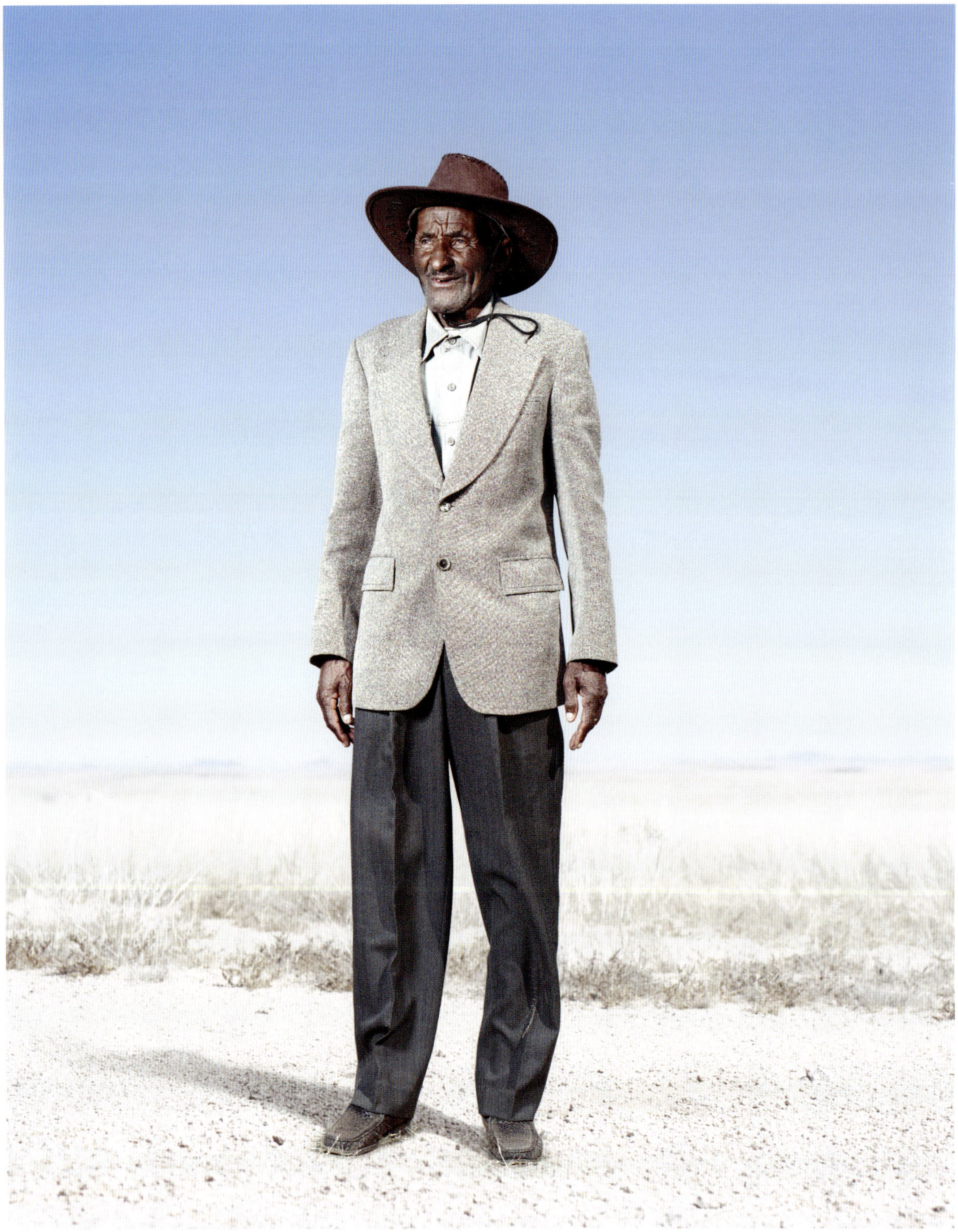

Male Herero headgear draws on a variety of sources. These men (above and opposite) are wearing cowboy hats, although the majority opt for the trilby.

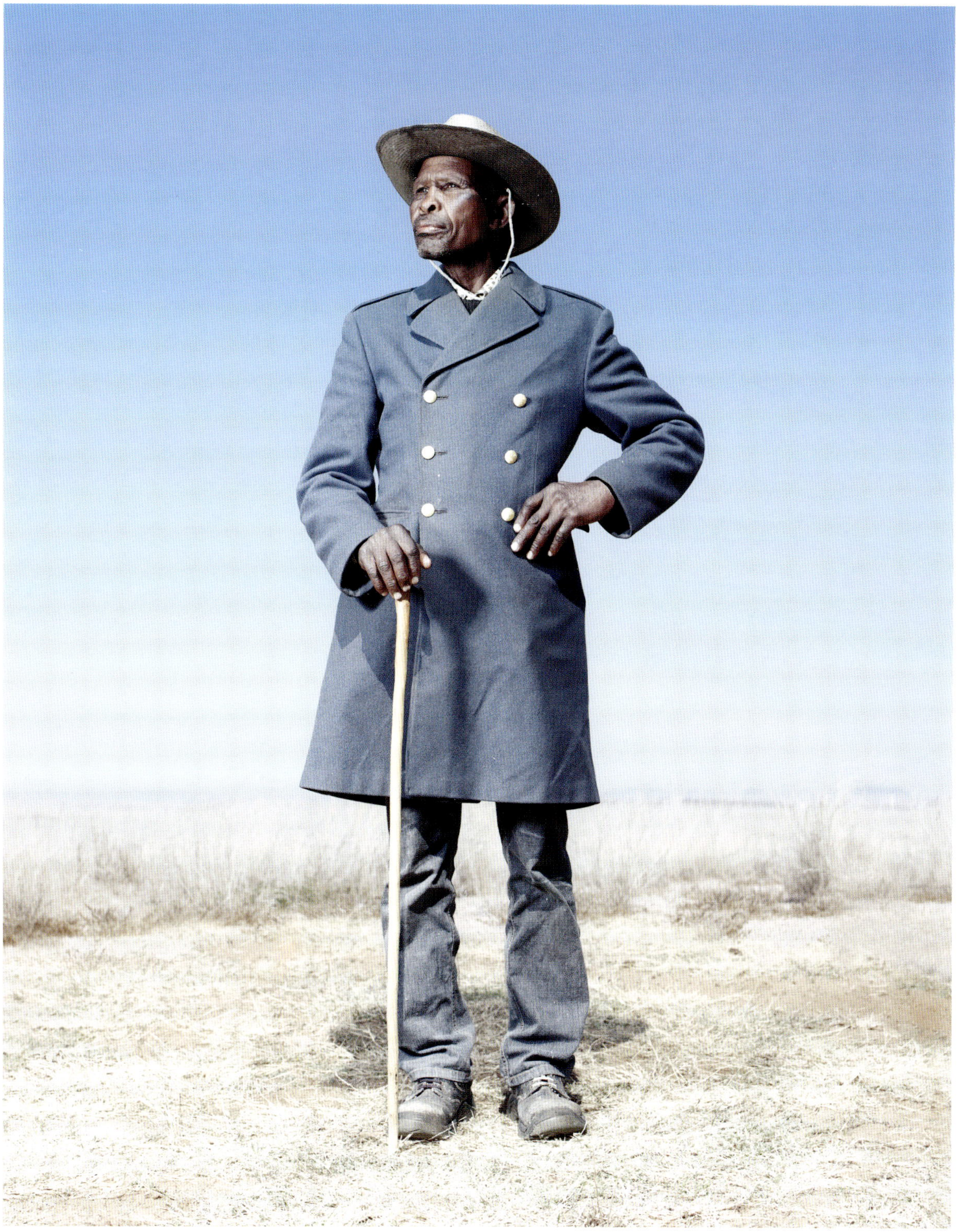

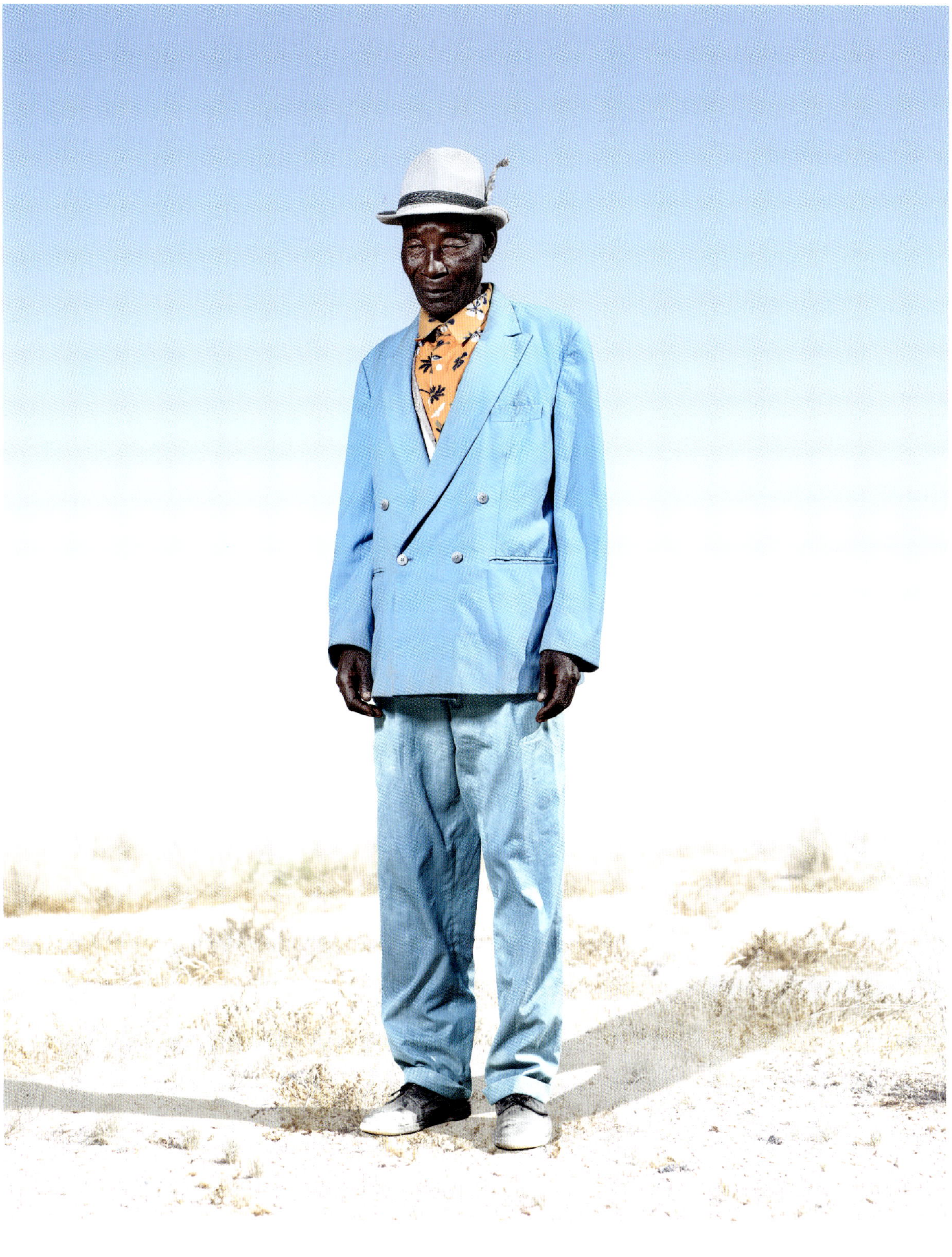

A Herero man in blue double-breasted suit.

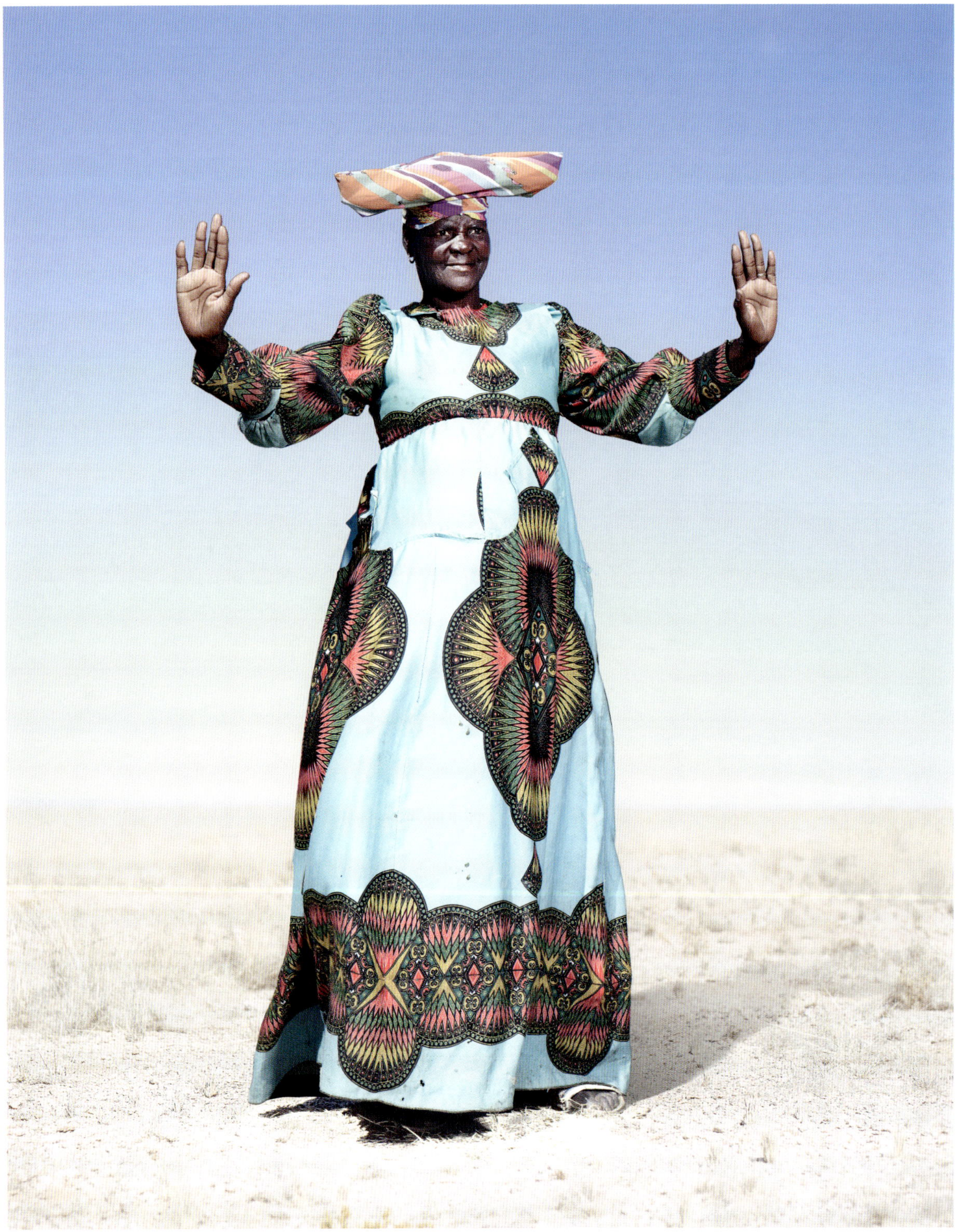

A Herero woman holds the pose of the cow dance (see page 23). Her arms, echoing the shape of her headdress, are bent to resemble a pair of horns.

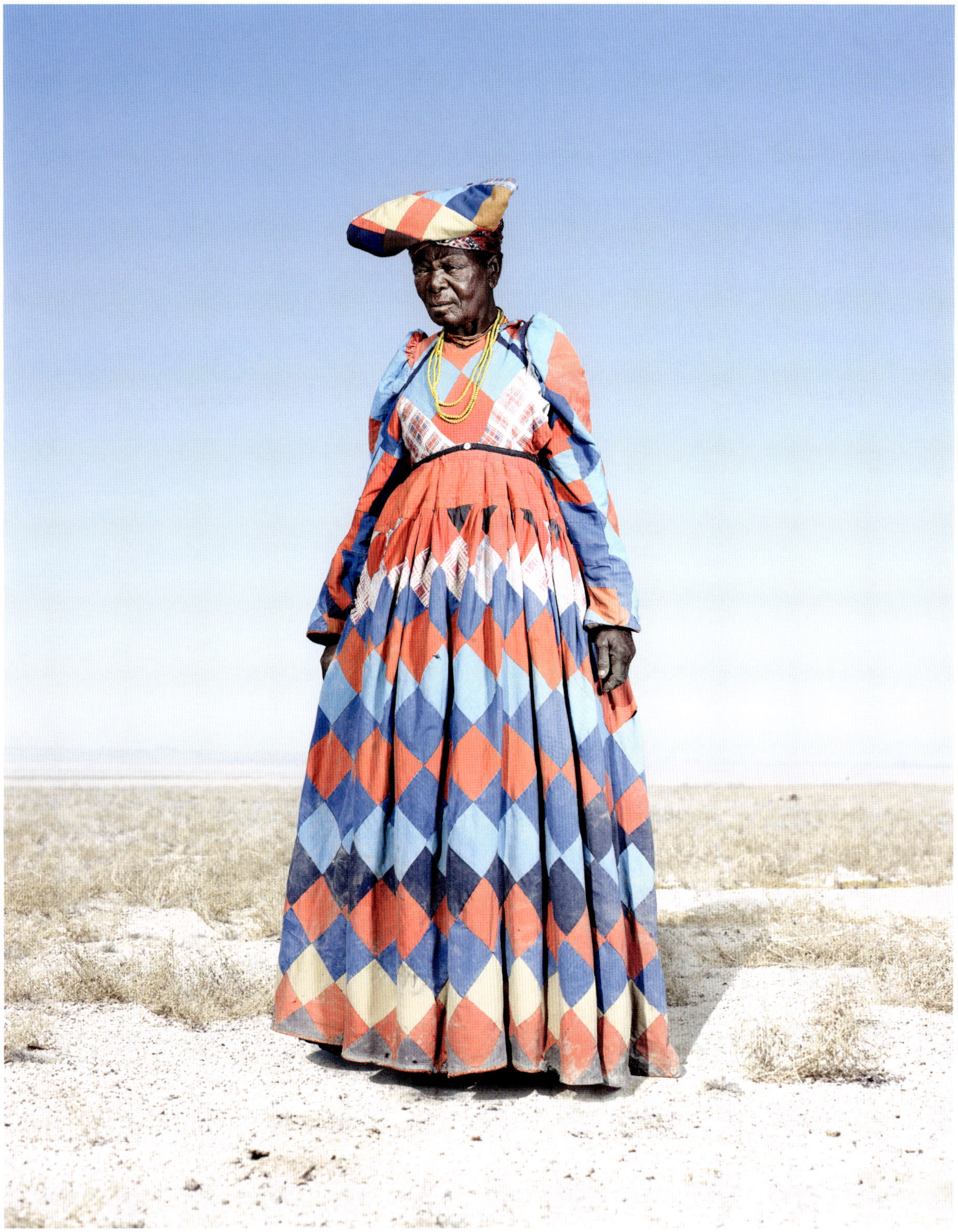

An elderly Herero woman in a diamond-patterned long dress.

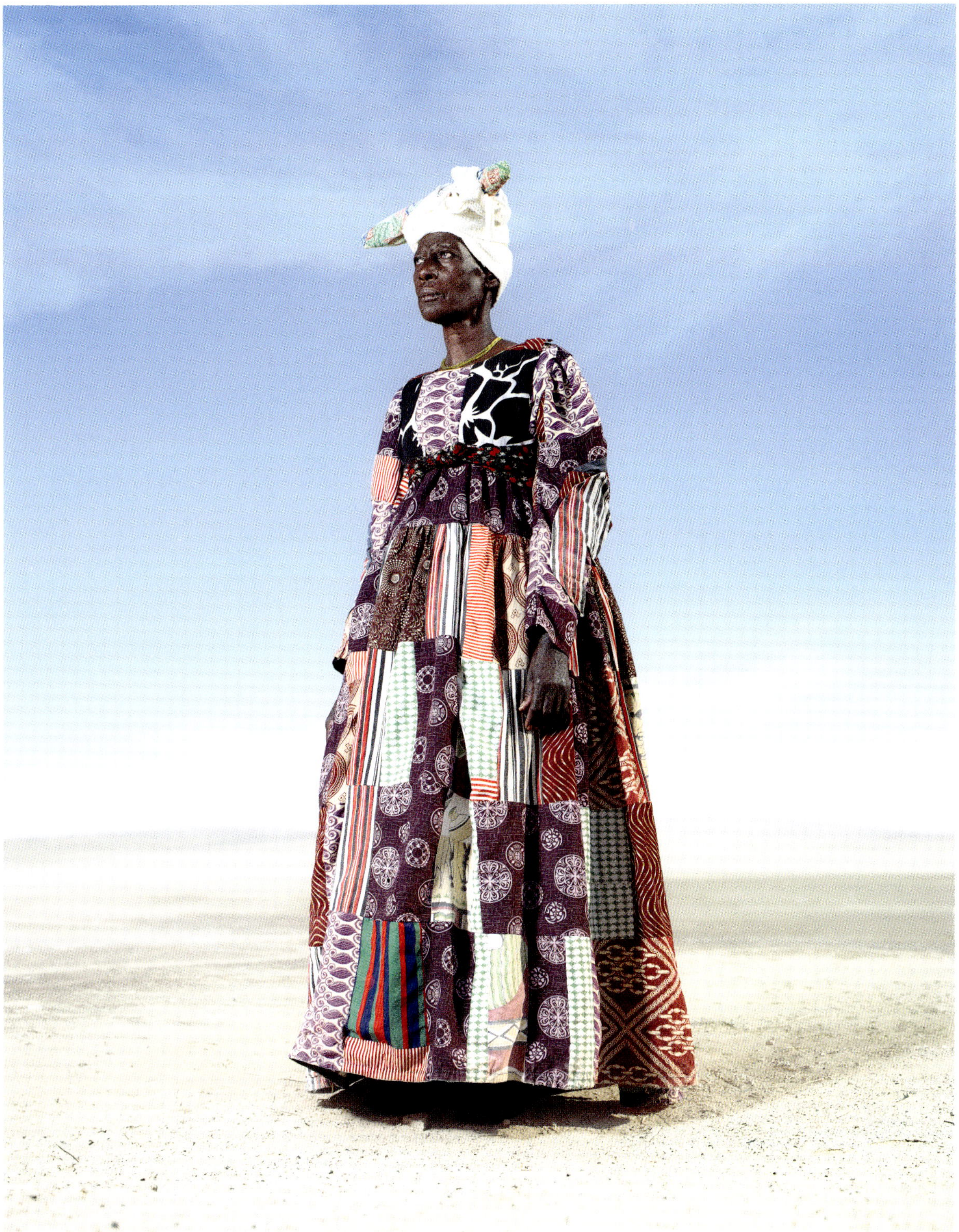

In common with this Herero woman, whose eyes are blue, some Hereros carry genes that have been passed down from the early period of German settlement.

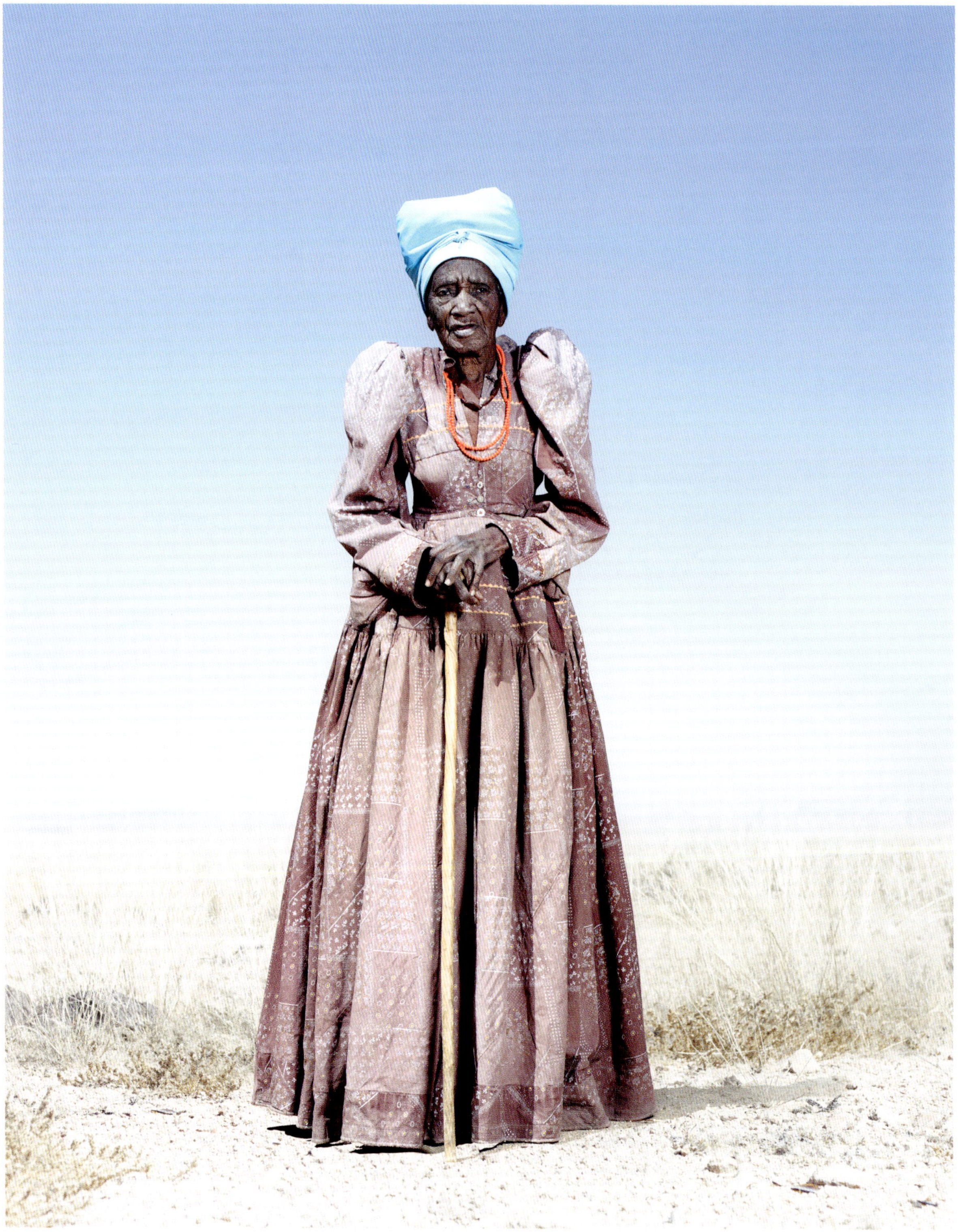

As is traditional, this Herero woman's advanced age is reflected in the size of her headdress (see page 39).

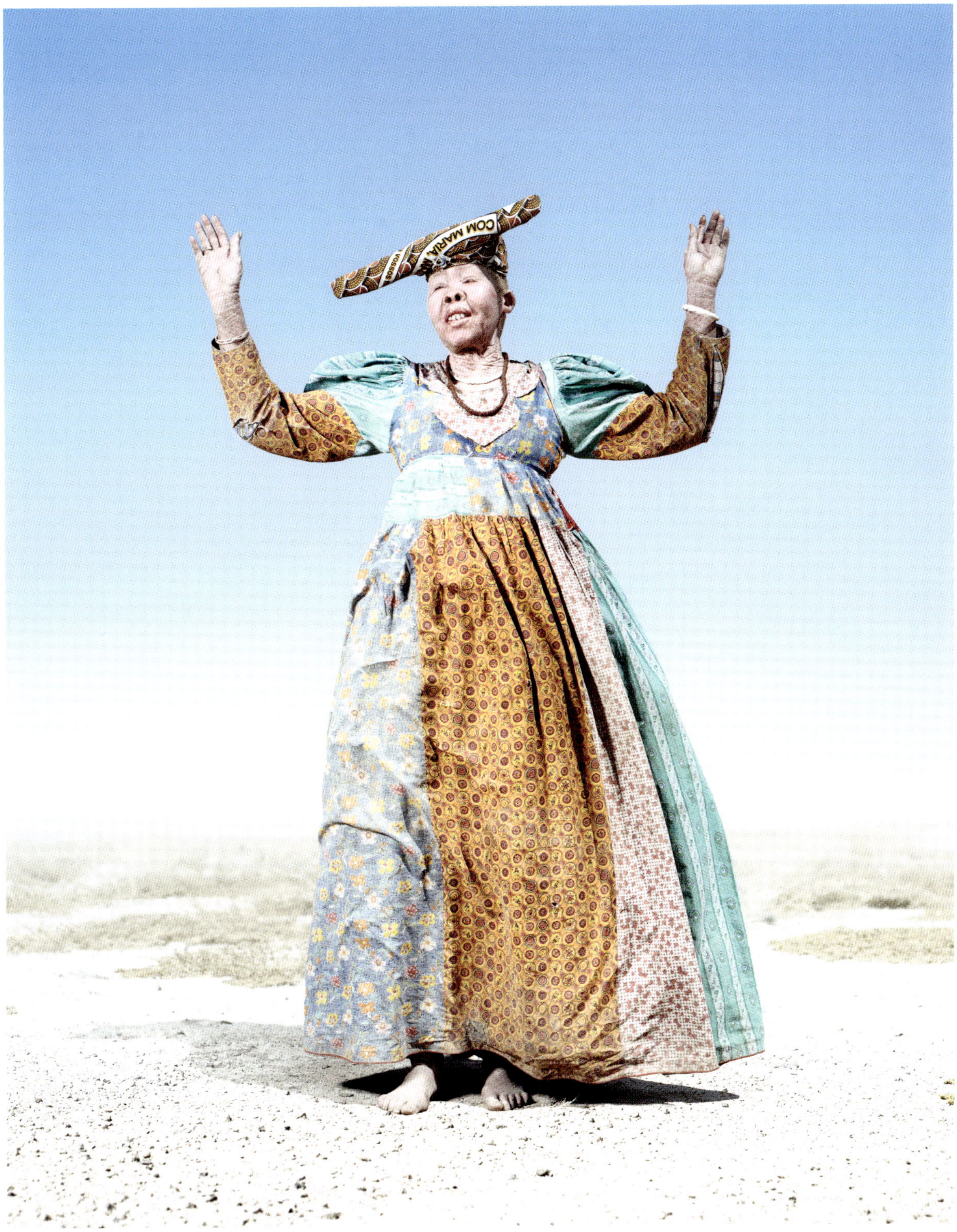

An albino Herero woman holding the cow-dance pose.

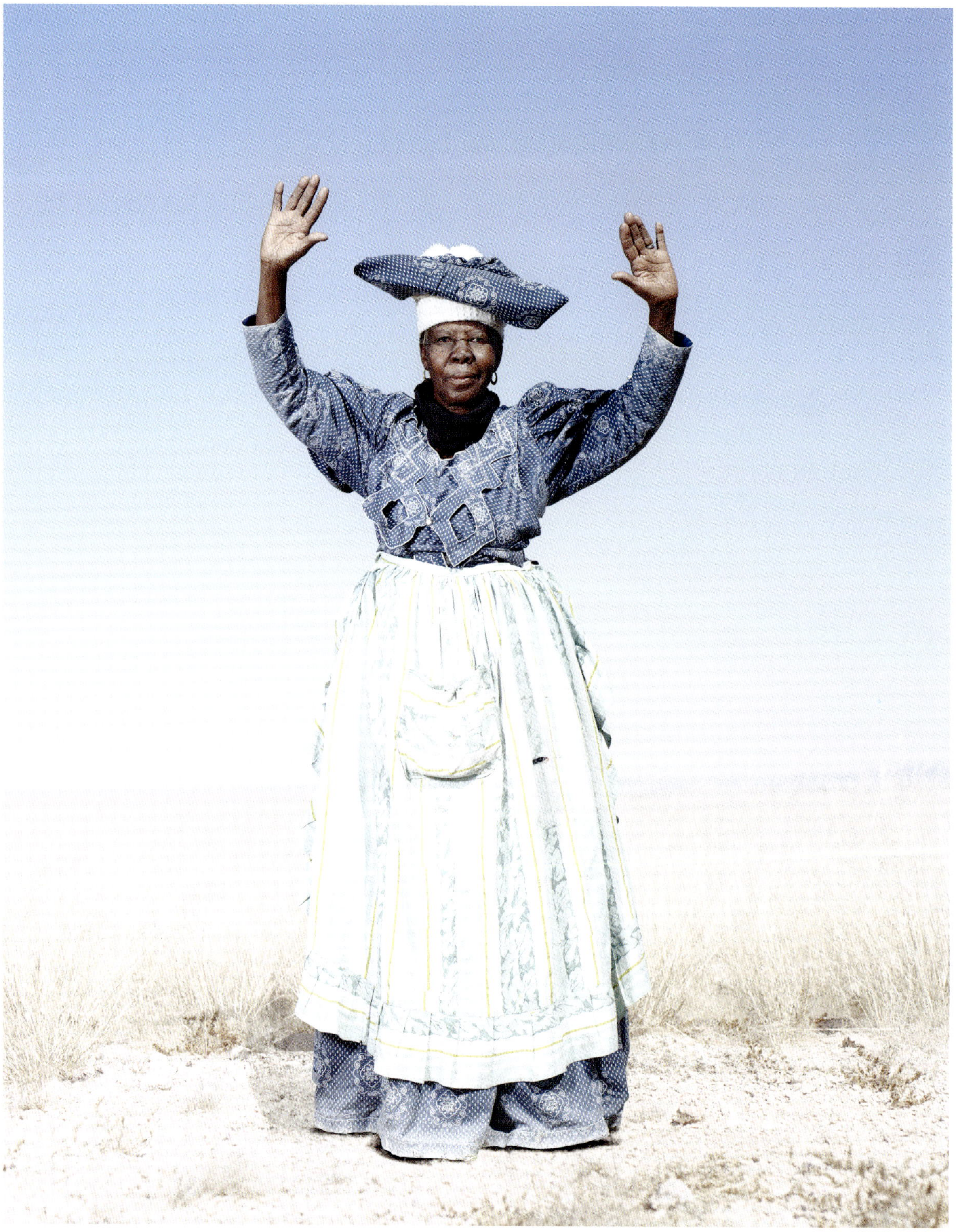

Two Herero women (above and opposite) assume
the pose of the cow dance. During the dance,
participants stamp their feet and kick up
dust in the manner of a bull.

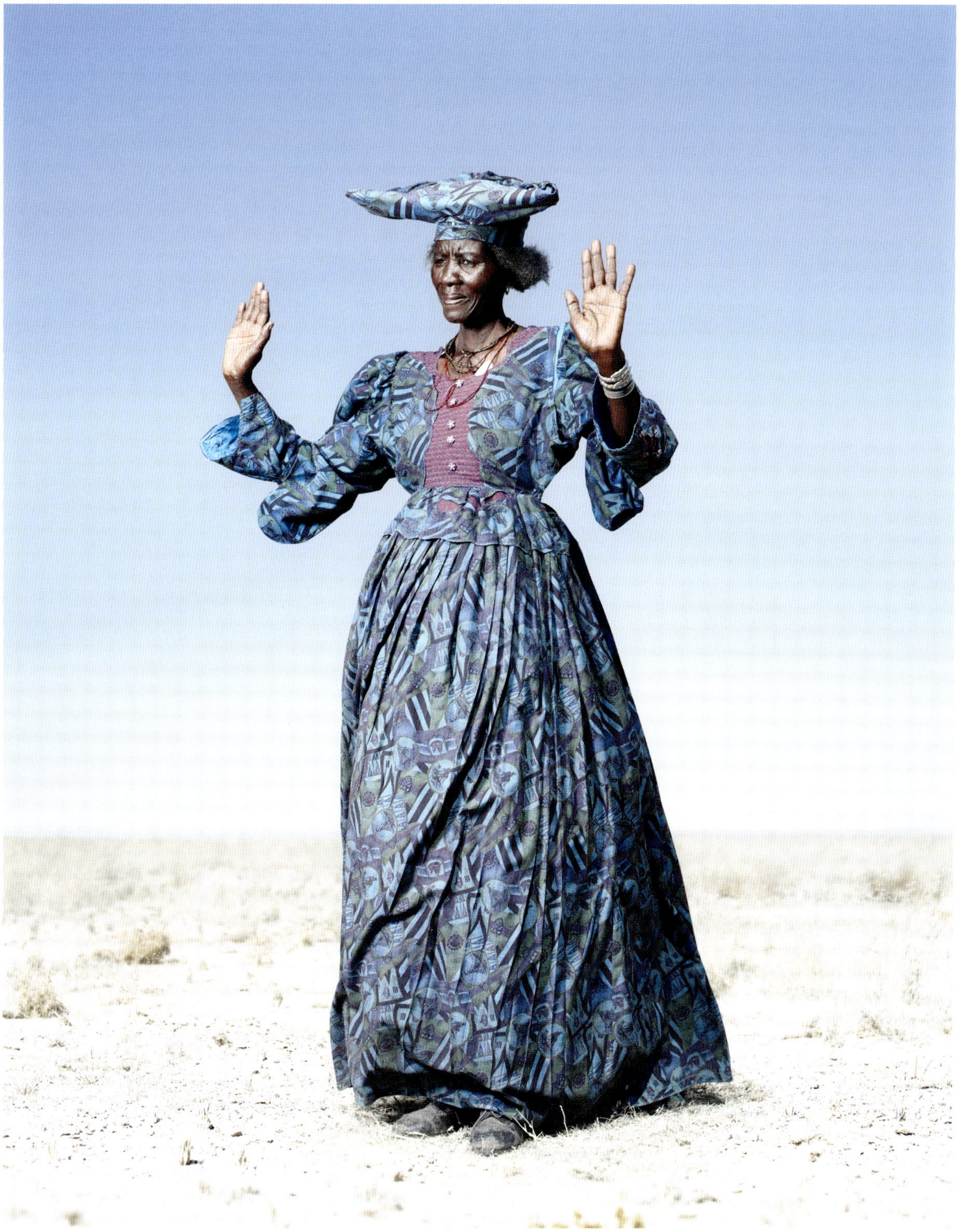

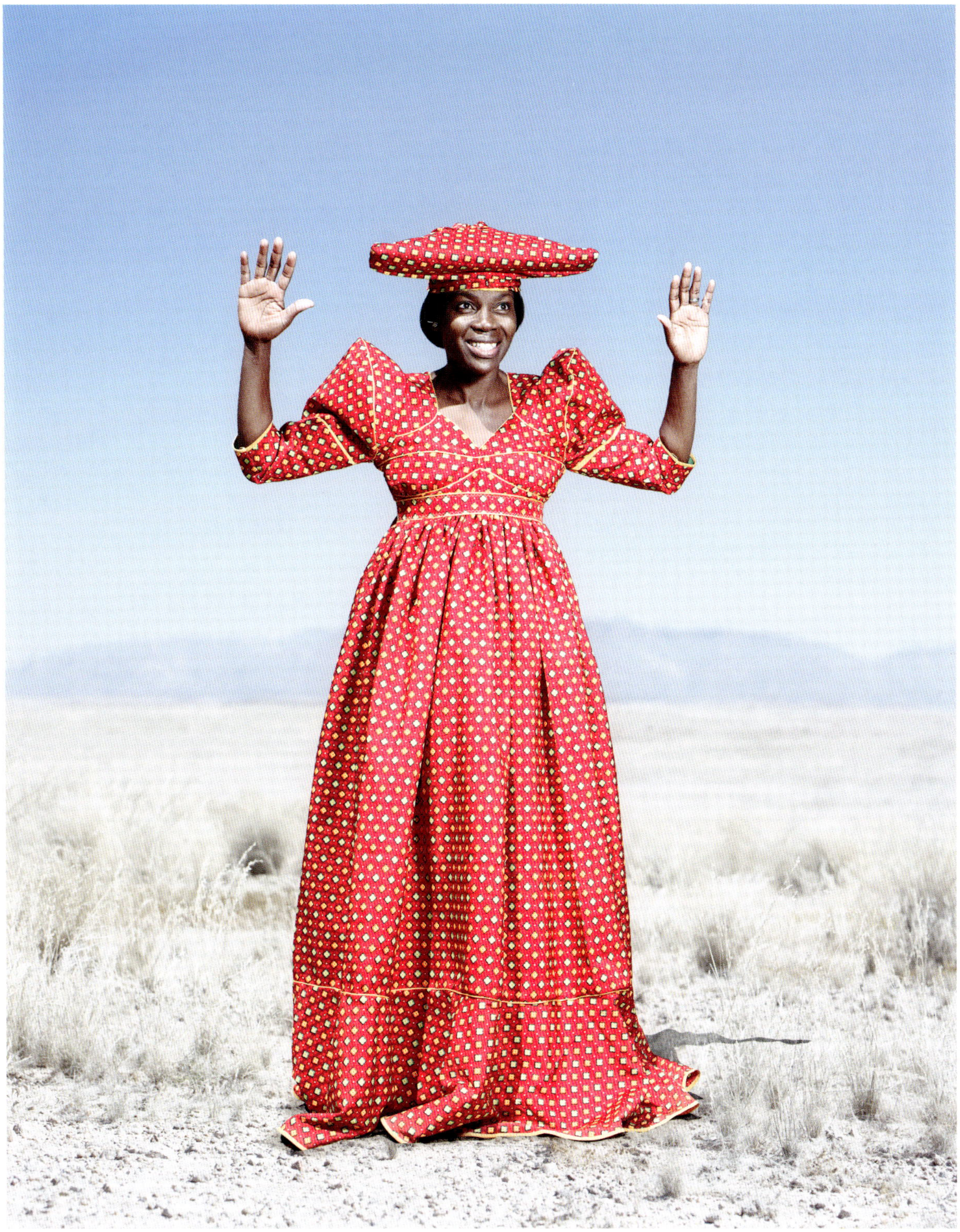

A Herero woman in a patterned long dress holds the cow-dance pose. According to Herero custom, the long dress should cover the wearer's feet, giving the illusion of gliding as they walk.

Further Reading

Jan-Bart Gewald, *Herero Heroes: A Socio-political History of the Herero of Namibia 1890–1923*, Oxford (James Currey) 1999

Hildi Hendrickson, 'The "Long" Dress and the Construction of Herero Identities in Southern Africa', *African Studies*, 53, 1994, pp. 25–54

Jekura U. Kavari, *The Form and Meaning of Otjiherero Praises*, Cologne (Rüdiger Köppe) 2002

Gesine Krüger and Dag Henrichsen, '"We Have Been Captives Long Enough. We Want to Be Free": Land, Uniforms and Politics in the History of the Herero in the Interwar Period', in *Namibia under South African Rule: Mobility and Containment, 1915–46*, ed. Patricia Hayes *et al.*, Oxford (James Currey) 1998, pp. 149–74

David Olusoga and Caspar W. Erichsen, *The Kaiser's Holocaust: Germany's Forgotten Genocide and the Colonial Roots of Nazism*, London (Faber & Faber) 2010

Wolfgang Werner, '"Playing Soldiers": The Truppenspieler Movement among the Herero of Namibia, 1915 to *c.* 1945', *Journal of Southern African Studies*, 16, 1990, pp. 485–502

Acknowledgements

I should like to thank Tim Ashton, Ken Ideus, Tarnia Kapow, K.K. Mahuka, Daniel Morgan and Ubald Rutar, without whose valuable assistance this book would not have been possible.

First published 2013 by Merrell Publishers, London and New York

Merrell Publishers Limited
81 Southwark Street
London SE1 0HX

merrellpublishers.com

Preface and captions copyright © 2013 Jim Naughten
Illustrations copyright © 2013 Jim Naughten;
for exceptions, see below
Introduction copyright © 2013 Merrell Publishers Limited
Design and layout copyright © 2013 Merrell Publishers Limited

All rights reserved. No part of this publication may be reproduced, stored in a retrieval system or transmitted, in any form or by any means, electronic, mechanical, photocopying, recording or otherwise, without the prior written permission of the publisher.

British Library Cataloguing-in-Publication Data. A catalogue record for this book is available from the British Library.

ISBN 978-1-8589-4600-9

Produced by Merrell Publishers Limited
Designed by Nicola Bailey
Project-managed by Mark Ralph

Printed and bound in China

PICTURE CREDITS
Pages 8, 14 and 15: Photo: akg-images.
Page 17: Photographer unknown. Basler Afrika Bibliographien, Fritz Gaerdes Collection, Image G20_0001.
© Basler Afrika Bibliographien.

JACKET, FRONT: See page 39.

JACKET, BACK: See page 80.

PAGE 1: A Herero woman in a pink floral-patterned long dress, matching headdress and yellow scarf. The muted tones of the Victorian-era clothing adopted by the Herero in the second half of the nineteenth century have long been rejected in favour of bright colours and strong patterns.

PAGES 10–11: Soldiers from the *Otjiserandu*, or 'Red Flag', section of the *Otruppe* march behind a flag-bearer. Marching displays are a feature of the annual Herero Day held in Okahandja (see page 62), but can also be seen all over the country, at funerals, meetings and other festivals and ceremonies.

OVERLEAF: A young *Otruppe* cadet. His uniform, in common with those of many *Otruppe* members, consists of a mixture of styles.

9 781858 946009

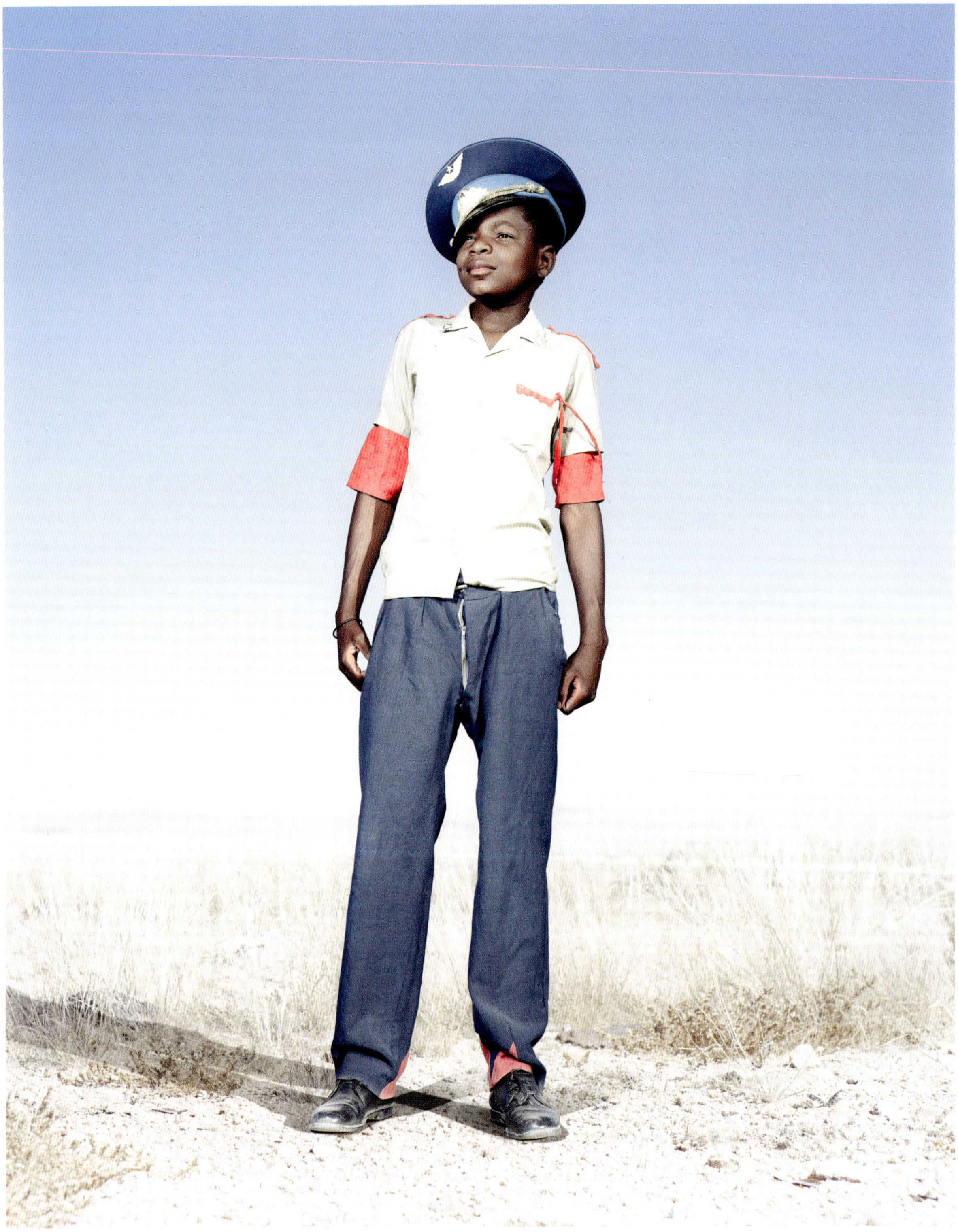